2010
Official Playing Rules
of the
National Football League

D0189085

TRIUMPH
B O O K S

Triumph Books and colophon are registered trademarks of Random House, Inc.

This cover and design treatment copyright © Triumph Books.
Design by Sue Knopf; page production by Patricia Frey.

This book is available at special discounts for your group or organization. For further information, contact:

Triumph Books
542 South Dearborn Street, Suite 750
Chicago, Illinois 60605
Tel: (312) 939-3330
Fax: (312) 663-3557
www.triumphbooks.com

Cover image courtesy of AP Images.

ISBN: 978-1-60078-417-0

PRINTED IN USA

Contents

User's Guide

This edition of the *Official Playing Rules of the National Football League* contains all current rules governing the playing of professional football that are in effect for the 2010 NFL season. Member clubs of the League may amend the rules from time to time, pursuant to the applicable voting procedures of the NFL Constitution and Bylaws.

Any intra-League dispute or call for interpretation in connection with these rules will be decided by the Commissioner of the League, whose ruling will be final.

Because interconference games are played throughout the preseason, regular season, and postseason in the NFL, all rules contained in this book apply uniformly to both the American and National Football Conferences.

At many places in the text there are approved rulings which serve to supplement and illustrate the basic language of the rules. Each is headed by an abbreviation, followed by a number (e.g. "**A.R. 32.0**"). The letter "A" in an approved ruling indicates the team that puts the ball in play, and its opponents are designated by the letter "B". Whenever a team is in possession of the ball, it is the offense, and at such time its opponent is the defense. Yard lines and players are indicated by numerals. Thus, for example: "**A.R. 50.1** Third-and-10 on A30. During a run prior to an intended pass by quarterback A1, defensive player B1 holds flanker A2 on the A45…"

Where the word "illegal" appears in this rule book, it is an institutional term of art pertaining strictly to actions that violate NFL playing rules. It is not meant to connote illegality under any public law or the rules or regulations of any other organization.

The word "flagrant," when used here to describe an action by a player, is meant to indicate the degree of a violation of the rules—usually a personal foul or unnecessary roughness—is extremely objectionable and conspicuous. "Flagrant" in these rules does not necessarily imply malice on the part of the fouling player or an intention to injure an opponent.

 Penalties are marked throughout the text with this icon.

New rules and changes to rules are underlined. Additionally, Rule 12 and Rule 16 have been substantially updated.

The Field

Rule 1

The Field

Section 1   **DIMENSIONS**   The game shall be played upon a rectangular field, 360 feet in length and 160 feet in width. The lines at each end of the field are termed End Lines. Those on each side are termed Sidelines. Goal Lines shall be established in the field 10 yards from and parallel to each end line. The area bounded by goal lines and sidelines is known as the Field of Play. The areas bounded by goal lines, end lines, and sidelines are known as the End Zones.

The areas bounded by goal lines and lines parallel to, and 70 feet 9 inches inbounds, from each sideline, are known as the Side Zones. The lines parallel to sidelines are termed Inbound Lines. The end lines and the sidelines are also termed Boundary Lines.

The playing field will be rimmed by a solid white border a minimum of 6 feet wide along the end lines and sidelines. An additional broken limit line 6 feet further outside this border is to encompass the playing field in the non-bench areas, and such broken line will be continued at an angle from each 32-yard line and pass behind the bench areas (all benches a minimum 30 feet back from the sidelines). In addition, within each bench area, a yellow line 6 feet behind the solid white border will delineate a special area for coaches, behind which all players, except one player charting the game, must remain. If a club's solid white border is a minimum of 12 feet wide, there is no requirement that the broken restraining line also be added in the non-bench areas. However, the appropriate yellow line described above must be clearly marked within the bench areas.

In special circumstances (for example, an artificial surface in a multi-purpose stadium) and subject to prior approval from the League Office, a club may omit the 6-foot solid white border during the preseason or later period while football overlaps with another sport, and substitute a single 4-inch white line at what normally would be the outer limit of the solid border (6 feet from the sidelines).

Section 2   **MARKINGS**   At intervals of 5 yards, yard lines (3-42-2) parallel to the goal lines shall be marked in the field of play. *These lines are to stop 8 inches short of the 6-foot solid border.* The 4-inch wide yard lines are to be extended 4 inches beyond the white 6-foot border along the sidelines. Each of these lines shall be intersected at right angles by short lines 70 feet, 9 inches long (23 yards, 1 foot, 9 inches) in from each side to indicate inbounds lines.

In line with the Inbound Lines there shall be marks at 1-yard intervals between each distance of 5 yards for the full length of the field. These lines are to begin 8 inches from the 6-foot solid border and are to measure 2 feet in length.

Bottoms of numbers indicating yard lines in multiples of 10 must be placed beginning 12 yards in from each sideline. These are to be 2 yards in length.

Two yards from the middle of each goal line and parallel to it, there shall be marked in the Field of Play, lines 1 yard in length.

All boundary lines, goal lines, and marked lines are to be continuous lines. These, and any other specified markings, must be in white, and there shall be no exceptions without authorization of the Commissioner. Field numerals must also be white.

Care must be exercised in any end-zone marking or decoration or club identification at the 50-yard line that said marking or decorations do not in any way cause confusion as to delineation of goal lines, sidelines, and end lines. Such markings or decorations must be approved by the Commissioner.

The four intersections of goal lines and sidelines must be marked, at inside corners, by weighted pylons. In addition, two such pylons shall be placed on each end line (four in all).

■ Supplemental Notes

All measurements are to be made from the inside edges of the line marking the boundary lines. Each goal line marking is to be in its end zone so that the edge of the line toward the field of play (actual goal line) is 30 feet from the inside edge of the end line. Each goal line is to be eight inches wide.

All lines are to be marked with a material that is not injurious to eyes or skin. It is desirable that the yard line markers be flexible in order to prevent injury. No benches or rigid fixtures should be nearer than 10 yards from sidelines.

In league parks where ground rules are necessary, because of fixed conditions that can not be changed, they will be made by the Commissioner. Otherwise they will be made by mutual agreement of the two coaches. If they cannot agree, the Referee is the final authority after consulting his crew.

Section 3   **GOAL**   In the plane of each end line there shall be a centrally placed horizontal Crossbar 18 feet 6 inches in length, the top face of which is 10 feet above the ground. The goal is the **vertical plane** extending indefinitely above the crossbar and between the lines indicated by the outer edges of the goal posts.

All goal posts will be the single-standard type, offset from the end line and bright gold in color. The uprights will extend 30 feet above the crossbar and will be no less than 3 inches and no more than 4 inches in diameter. An orange-colored ribbon 4 inches by 42 inches is to be attached to the top of each post.

Note: Goal posts must be padded in a manner prescribed by the league.

Section 4   **PLAYERS' BENCHES**   At the option of the home team, both the players' benches may be located on the same side of the field. In such a case, the end of each bench shall start at the 45-yard line and continue towards the adjacent goal line.

Note: When both benches are so located, chain crew and linesmen are to operate during entire game on opposite side to benches. See 15-4-1.

Section 5   **CHAIN CREW AND BALL BOYS**   Members of the chain crew and the ball boys must be uniformly identifiable as specified by the Commissioner. White shirts are to be worn by members of the chain crew.

Section 6   **SIDELINE MARKERS**   The home club must provide and use the standard set of sideline markers that have been approved by the Commissioner.

Plan of the Playing Field

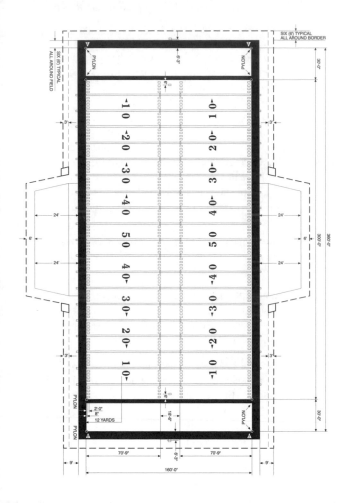

Field Markings

1. The playing field will be rimmed by a solid white border six feet wide along the end lines and sidelines. There will be an additional broken yellow line nine feet farther outside this border along each sideline in the non-bench areas, and such broken line will be continued at an angle from each 30-yard line and pass behind the bench area (all benches a minimum of 30 feet back from the sidelines) at a distance of six feet. In each end zone, this broken yellow line is six feet from the solid white border. These yellow broken lines are to be eight inches wide and two feet long with a space of one foot between them.

In addition, within each bench area, a solid yellow line six feet behind the solid border will delineate a special area for coaches, behind which all players, except one player who is charting the game, must remain. Furthermore, a broken white line four inches wide and four feet long with a space of two-foot intervals will be marked three feet inside the nine-foot restriction line on the sideline, extending to meet the existing yellow broken line six feet behind both end zones and at each television box outside the bench area.

2. All lines are to be four inches wide, with the exception of the goal line and yellow lines, which are to be eight inches wide. Tolerance of line widths is plus one-fourth inch.

Inbound Yard Markers

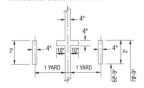

Dimensions for Numerals on the Playing Field

Dimensions for the Directional Arrows

3. All line work is to be laid out to dimensions shown on the plan with a tolerance of plus one-fourth inch. All lines are straight.

4. All boundary lines, goal lines, and marked yard lines are to be continuous lines.

5. The four intersections of goal lines and sidelines must be marked at inside corners of the end zone and the goal line by pylons. Pylons must be placed at inside edges of white lines and should not touch the surface of the actual playing field itself.

6. All lines are to be marked with a material that is not injurious to eyes or skin.

7. No benches or rigid fixtures should be nearer than 10 yards from the sidelines. If space permits, they may be further back.

8. Player benches can be situated anywhere between respective 35-yard lines. Where possible, a continuation of the dotted yellow line is to extend from the 30-yard lines to a point six feet behind the player benches thereby enclosing this area.

9. A white arrow is to be placed on the ground adjacent to the top portion of each number (with the exception of the 50) with the point formed by the two longer sides pointing toward the goal line. The two longer sides measure 36 inches each, while the crossfield side measures 18 inches. The 18-inch crossfield side is to start 15 inches below the top, and 6 inches from the goalward edge of each outer number (except the 50).

10. The location of the inbounds lines is 70'9" for professional football, 60'0" for college football. On fields used primarily by the NFL, the professional inbounds lines should be 4 inches wide by 2 feet long. Alternate college lines, if they are to be included, should be 4 inches wide by 1 foot long.

11. Care must be exercised in any end zone marking, decoration, or club identification at the 50-yard line, that said marks or decorations do not in any way cause confusion as to delineation of goal lines, sidelines, and end lines. Such markings or decorations must be approved by the Commissioner.

NFL Bench Area Showing Restricting Zones

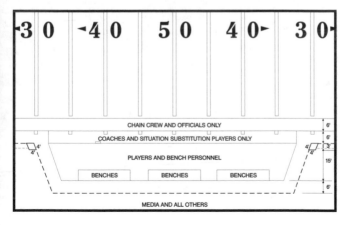

The Ball

Rule 2

The Ball

Section 1   The Ball must be a "Wilson," hand selected, bearing the signature of the Commissioner of the league, Roger Goodell.

The ball shall be made up of an inflated ($12\frac{1}{2}$ to $13\frac{1}{2}$ pounds) urethane bladder enclosed in a pebble grained, leather case (natural tan color) without corrugations of any kind. It shall have the form of a prolate spheroid and the size and weight shall be: long axis, 11 to $11\frac{1}{4}$ inches; long circumference, 28 to $28\frac{1}{2}$ inches; short circumference, 21 to $21\frac{1}{4}$ inches; weight, 14 to 15 ounces.

The Referee shall be the sole judge as to whether all balls offered for play comply with these specifications. A pump is to be furnished by the home club, and balls shall remain under the supervision of the Referee until they are delivered to the ball attendant just prior to the start of the game.

Section 2   Each team will make 12 primary balls available for testing by the Referee two hours and 15 minutes prior to the starting time of the game to meet League requirements. The home team will also make 12 backup balls available for testing in <u>all</u> stadiums. In addition, the visitors, at their discretion, may bring 12 backup balls to be tested by the Referee for games held in outdoor stadiums. For games in outdoor stadiums, eight new footballs, sealed in a special box and shipped by the manufacturer to the Referee, will be opened in the officials' locker room two hours and 15 minutes prior to the starting time of the game. These balls are to be specially marked by the Referee and used exclusively for the kicking game. For games in indoor stadiums, six new footballs will be shipped.

In the event a home team ball does not conform to specifications, or its supply is exhausted, the Referee shall secure a proper ball from visitors and, failing that, use the best available ball. Any such circumstances must be reported to the Commissioner.

In case of rain or a wet, muddy, or slippery field, a playable ball shall be used at the request of the offensive team's center. The Game Clock shall not stop for such action (unless undue delay occurs).

Note: It is the responsibility of the home team to furnish playable balls at all times by attendants from either side of the playing field.

Definitions

Rule 3

Definitions

Section 1   **APPROVED RULING (A.R.)**

An Approved Ruling (A.R.) is an official decision on a given statement of facts and serves to illustrate the intent, application, or amplification of a rule. Supplemental notes are often used for the same purpose (3-33).

An Official Ruling (O.R.) is a ruling made by the Interpretation Committee in the interim between the annual rules meeting and is official only during the current season.

Technical Terms are such terms that have a fixed and exact meaning throughout the code. Because of their alphabetical arrangement in Rule 3, certain ones are used prior to being defined. In such cases they are accented only the first time they are used.

Section 2   **BALL IN PLAY, DEAD BALL**

Article 1   The Ball is in Play (or Live Ball) when it is:

    (a) legally free kicked (6-1-1), or

    (b) legally snapped (7-3-1).

It continues in play until the down ends (3-7-1; 7-4-1).

Article 2   A Dead Ball is one that is not in play. The time period during which the ball is dead is Between Downs. This includes the interval during all time outs (including intermission) and from the time the ball becomes dead until it is legally put in play.

Article 3   A Loose Ball is a live ball that is not in player **possession**, i.e., any **kick, pass,** or **fumble.** A loose ball that has not yet struck the ground is In Flight. A loose ball (either during or after flight) is considered in **possession** of team (**offense**) whose **player kicked, passed,** or **fumbled.** It ends when a player secures possession or when **down ends** if that is before such possession. (For exception, see 9-5-1-Exc. 3).

Article 4   A Fumble is any act, other than a pass or kick, which results in loss of player possession. The term Fumble always implies possession. (8-7-3).

Note: If a player pretends to fumble and causes the ball to go forward, it is a forward pass and may be illegal (8-1-2-Pen. a, c).

A.R. 3.1 While runner A1 is in possession, defensive player B1 grabs the ball away from him.
Ruling: Fumble.

A.R. 3.2 While runner A1 is in possession, defensive player B1 bats or kicks the ball away from him.
Ruling: A foul during a fumble. Kicking a ball in player possession is a foul (12-1-9).

Article 5   A Muff is the **touching** of the ball by a player in an unsuccessful attempt to obtain **possession** of a loose ball.

Note: Any ball intentionally muffed forward is a bat and may be a foul. (3-2-5-g; 12-1-8).

Touching the Ball refers to any contact. Ordinarily there is no distinction between a player touching the ball with his hands or any part of his body being touched by it except as specifically provided for (3-15-3-Note 1 and 9-2-4).

Note: The result of the touching is sometimes influenced by the intent or the location.

(a) See 6-1-4-c and 6-2-4 for touching a free kick.

(b) See 6-4-1 for touching a free kick before it goes **out of bounds** between the goal lines.

(c) See 8-1-8 for **ineligible offensive player** touching a forward pass **on, behind,** or **beyond** the line.

(d) See 9-2 for touching a scrimmage kick on or behind the line, and also 9-2-4 for being pushed into a kick by an opponent.

(e) See 11-4-2 for touching a kick during an attempted **field goal.**

(f) Simultaneous touching by two opponents of a fumble, pass, or kick is treated under their respective sections.

(g) A Bat or Punch is the intentional striking of the ball with hand, fist, elbow, or forearm. See 12-1-8.

Article 6   A player (5-2-2) is inbounds when he first touches both feet or any other part of his body, other than his hands, to the ground within the boundary lines (1-1). See (3-21-1) for a player out of bounds.

Note: Unless otherwise stated in the Rules, a player is deemed to be inbounds.

Article 7   A player is in possession when he is in firm grip and control of the ball inbounds (See 3-2-3).

To gain possession of a loose ball (3-2-3) that has been caught, intercepted, or recovered, a player must have complete control of the ball and have both feet completely on the ground inbounds or any other part of his body, other than his hands, on the ground inbounds. If the player loses the ball while simultaneously touching both feet or any other part of his body to the ground or if there is any doubt that the acts were simultaneous, there is no possession. This rule applies in the field of play and in the end zone.

The terms catch, intercept, recover, advance, and fumble denote player possession (as distinguished from touching or muffing).

Note 1: A player who goes to the ground in the process of attempting to secure possession of a loose ball (with or without contact by <u>an opponent</u>) must maintain control of the ball after he touches the ground, whether in the field of play or the end zone. If he loses control of the ball, and the ball touches the ground before he regains control, there is no possession. If he regains control prior to the ball touching the ground, it is a catch, interception, or recovery.

Note 2: If a player goes to the ground out-of-bounds (with or without contact by an opponent) in the process of attempting to secure possession of a loose ball at the sideline, he must retain complete and continuous control of the ball throughout the act of falling to the ground and after hitting the ground, or there is no possession.

Note 3: If a player has control of the ball, a slight move-ment of the ball will not be considered loss of possession. He must lose control of the ball in order to rule that there has been a loss of possession.

A catch is made when a player inbounds secures posses-sion of a pass, kick, or fumble in flight (See 8-1-3).

Note 1: It is a catch if in the process of attempting to catch the ball, a player secures control of the ball prior to the ball touching the ground and that control is maintained after the ball has touched the ground.

Note 2: In the field of play, if a catch of a forward pass has been completed, and there is contact by a defender causing the ball to come loose before the runner is down by contact, it is a fumble, and the ball remains alive. In the end zone, the same action is a touchdown, since the receiver completed the

---

catch beyond the goal line prior to the loss of possession, and the ball is dead when the catch is completed.

An interception is made when a pass (forward or backward) is caught by an opponent of the passer.

The term recover indicates securing possession of a loose ball by either the offense or defense after it has touched the ground.

Note 1: If there is any question by the covering official(s) as to whether a forward pass is complete, intercepted, or incomplete, it always will be ruled incomplete.

Note 2: Recovery does not imply advance, unless so stated.

Note 3: If a player would have caught, intercepted, or recovered a ball inbounds, but is carried out of bounds, player possession will be granted (8-1-3 item 6).

Section 3   BLOCKING

Blocking is the act of obstructing or impeding an opponent by contacting him with a part of the blocker's body.

A Block in the Back is a block that is delivered from behind an opponent above his waist. It is not a block in the back:

(a) if the opponent turns away from the blocker, or

(b) if both of the blocker's hands are on the opponent's side.

A Block Below the Waist is when the initial contact is below the waist with any part of the blocker's body against an opponent, other than the runner, who has one or both feet on the ground. A blocker who makes contact above the waist and then slides below the waist has not blocked below the waist.

Note: If an opponent uses his hands to ward off a block, and the blocker contacts the opponent below the waist, it is not a block below the waist unless the blocker is obviously intending to deliver a low block.

Section 4 CHUCKING

Chucking is a means of warding off an eligible receiver who is in front of a defender by contacting him with a quick extension of arm or arms followed by the return of arm(s) to a flexed position, or by maintaining continuous and unbroken contact within five yards of the line of scrimmage, so long as the receiver has not moved beyond the point that is even with the defender (See 8-4 Articles 1-4).

Section 5 CLIPPING

Clipping is throwing the body across the back of the leg of an eligible receiver or charging or falling into the back of an opponent below the waist after approaching him from behind, provided the opponent is not a *runner*.

Note: See 12-2-9 for additional interpretations or restrictions concerning clipping in close line play.

A.R. 3.3 Runner A1 advances 10 yards and is hit from behind by defensive player B1, who throws his body across the back of A1's leg.
Ruling: Legal and not a clip, because A1 was a runner. If A1 was not a runner, it would have been a clip.

Section 6 DISQUALIFIED PLAYER

A Disqualified Player is one who is banished from further participation in the game and must return to his dressing room within a reasonable period of time for any of the following:

(a) flagrant striking, kneeing, or kicking an opponent (12-2-1);

(b) flagrant roughing of a kicker, passer, or any other opponent (12-2-6 and <u>12-2-13</u>);

(c) a palpably unfair act (12-3-3);

(d) flagrant unsportsmanlike conduct by players or non-players (Rule 13); or

(e) repeat violation of a suspended player rule (5-4-Pen. c).

Note: Disqualified player is not to reappear in his team uniform nor return to any area other than to which spectators have access.

Section 7   DOWN

Article 1   A Down is a period of action that starts when the ball is put in play (3-2-1) and ends when ball is next dead (7-4-1).

A down that starts with a snap is known as a Scrimmage Down (3-30).

A down that starts with a fair catch kick is known as a fair catch kick down (10-2-4; 11-4-3).

A down that starts with a free kick is known as a Free Kick Down (6-1-1).

Article 2   A Series of Downs is the four consecutive charged scrimmage downs allotted to the offensive team during which it must advance the ball to a yard line called the necessary line in order to retain possession (7-1-1).

The Necessary Line is always 10 yards in advance of the spot of the snap (which starts the series) except when a goal line is less than 10 yards from this spot. In that case the necessary line is the goal line.

When the offensive team has been in possession constantly during a scrimmage down, the down is counted as one of a series except as provided for a foul (14-8), and is known as a Charged Down.

The initial down in each series is known as the First Down, and if it is a charged down, subsequent charged downs are numbered consecutively until a new series is declared for either team (7-1-1).

Section 8   **DROP KICK**

A Drop Kick is a kick by a kicker who drops the ball and kicks it as, or immediately after, it touches the ground.

Section 9   **FAIR CATCH**

A Fair Catch is an unhindered catch by any player of the receivers of a free kick or of a scrimmage kick except one that has not crossed the line of scrimmage (3-18-3), provided he has legally signaled his intention of attempting such a catch (10-2-2-Item 1).

Article 1   The Mark of the Catch is the spot from either:

(a) where the ball is actually caught by a receiver after a fair catch signal, valid or invalid (10-2-2); or

(b) the spot of ball after a penalty for fair catch interference (10-1-1-Pen. b), and after a penalty for running into the maker of a fair catch (10-2-3-c).

Note: For fair catch kick, see 10-2-4-a and 11-4-3.

Section 10   **FIELD GOAL**

A Field Goal is made by kicking the ball from the field of play through the plane of the opponents' goal by a drop kick or a placekick either:

(a) From behind the line on a play from scrimmage; or

(b) During a fair catch kick. See 11-4-3; 3-9; and 10-2-4-a.

Section 11   FOUL AND SPOTS OF ENFORCEMENT

Article 1   A Foul is any infraction of a playing rule. Spot of Enforcement (or Basic Spot) is the *spot* at which a *penalty* is *enforced.* Four such spots are commonly used (14-1). They are:

(a) Spot of Foul—The spot where a foul was committed or is so considered by rule.

(b) Previous Spot—The identical spot where the ball was last put in play.

(c) Spot of Snap, backward pass, or fumble—The spot where the foul occurred or the spot where the penalty is to be enforced.

(d) Succeeding Spot—The spot where the ball would next be put in play if no distance penalty were to be enforced.

Note: After a penalty enforcement, the ball is next put in play at the nearest inbounds line if the penalty enforcement would leave the ball outside the inbounds line.

Exception: If a foul occurs after a touchdown and before the ready for play signal for a Try, the succeeding spot is the spot of the next kickoff.

Note: A penalty is never enforced from the spot of a legal kick from scrimmage (9-5-1).

An enforcement includes a declination (14-6). See 14-1-5 for definition of basic spot and 3 and 1 rule.

Article 2   **Types of Fouls**

(a) A Dead Ball Foul (or a subsequent foul) is a personal foul (12-2) or unsportsmanlike foul (12-3) that

---

occurs after a down ends and before the next snap or
free kick (14-5). See 14-1-7 to <u>14-1-10</u>.

*Note: A dead ball foul is always enforced from the succeed-
ing spot.*

(b) A Multiple Foul is two or more fouls by the same
team during the same down, unless they are part of a
double foul (14-4).

(c) A Double Foul is a foul by each team during the
same down and includes any multiple foul by either
team, including dead ball fouls (14-3).

A.R. 3.4 A's ball first-and-10 on A30. Runner A1 runs
out of bounds on the A45, after which offensive A2 clips
on the A30.
Ruling: A's ball first-and-10 on A30. A dead ball foul.
See 14-1-7. It happened after the down ended and was a
personal foul. See A.R. 14.56.

A.R. 3.5 Defensive B1 holds an offensive player on the
line of scrimmage. Defensive B2 was offside.
Ruling: A multiple foul because it was two fouls by the
same team during the same down. See 14-4.

A.R. 3.6 The offensive team is offside. The defensive
team interferes with an eligible receiver downfield. The
pass falls incomplete.
Ruling: A double foul because each team committed a
foul during the same down. See 14-3.

A.R. 3.7 The offensive team clips after Runner A1
scored.
Ruling: A foul between downs because the down ended
when the score was made. Penalize on subsequent
kickoff. See 14-1-7 and 14-5

Section 12   **FREE KICK**

Article 1   A Free Kick is one that puts the ball in play to start a
              free kick down (3-2-1, 6-1-1): It includes:

              (a) kickoff;

              (b) safety kick (6-1-1-b).

Article 2   The Free Kick Line for the kicking team is a yard line
              through the most forward point from which the ball is
              to be kicked (6-1-2-a).

              The Free Kick Line for the receiving team is a yard line
              10 yards in advance of the kicking team's free kick line
              (6-1-2-b).

Section 13   **HANDING THE BALL**

Article 1   Handing the ball is transferring player possession from
              one teammate to another without passing or kicking it.

              (a) Except where permitted by rule, handing the ball
                  forward to a teammate is illegal.

              (b) Loss of player possession by unsuccessful execution
                  of attempted handing is a fumble charged to the
                  player that last had possession.

              (c) A forward handoff occurs when the ball is handed
                  (regardless of the direction of the movement of the
                  ball) to a player who is in advance of a teammate
                  whose hands he takes or receives it.

              (d) A muffed handoff (legal or illegal) is a fumble, and
                  the ball remains alive.

Section 14   **HUDDLE**

              A Huddle is the action of two or more players of the
              offensive team who, instead of assuming their normal
              position for the snap, form a group for getting the signal
              for the next play or for any other reason.

Section 15 **IN TOUCH AND IMPETUS**

Article 1 A Ball is In Touch:

(a) after it has come from the field of play, it touches a goal line (plane) while in player possession; or

(b) while it is loose, it touches anything on or behind a goal line.

Note (1): If a player while standing on or behind the goal line touches a ball that has come from the field of play and the official is in doubt as to whether the ball actually touched the goal line (plane), he shall rule that the ball was in touch.

Note (2): A ball in the end zone which is carried toward the field of play is still in touch. It is a safety or touchback if any part of the ball is on, above, or behind the goal line (plane) when dead. In such a case, the ball must be entirely in the field of play in order not to be in touch.

Article 2 A Ball Dead in Touch is one dead on or behind a goal line and it is either a *touchdown,* a *safety,* a *touchback,* a *field goal,* or the termination of a *Try* (11-3), or a loss of down at the spot of the foul.

Note 1: Sometimes a safety, touchdown, or Try (unsuccessful) is awarded because of a foul. In such cases they are penalties.

Note 2: Momentum is an exception to dead in touch. See 11-5-1-Exc. 2

Article 3 Impetus is the action of a player that gives momentum to the ball and sends it in touch.

The Impetus is attributed to the offense except when the ball is sent in touch through a new momentum when the *defense* muffs a ball which is at rest, or nearly at rest, or illegally *bats:*

(a) a kick or fumble;

(b) a backward pass after it has struck <u>the</u> ground;

(c) or illegally kicks any ball (12-1-9).

Note 1: If a player is pushed or blocked into any kick or fumble or into a backward pass after it has struck <u>the</u> ground, and if such pushing or blocking is the primary factor that sends such a loose ball in touch, the impetus is by the pusher or blocker, and the pushed (blocked) player will not be considered to have touched the ball. See 9-2-4.

Note 2: Momentum is not applicable (11-5-1-Exc. 2).

Section 16 KICKER

A Kicker is the player of the offensive team who legally punts, placekicks, or dropkicks the ball. The offensive team is known as the Kickers during a kick.

A Receiver is any defensive player during a kick. The defensive team is known as the Receivers during a kick.

Section 17 KICKOFF

A Kickoff is a free kick used to put the ball in play:

(a) At start of the first and third periods;

(b) After each Try; and

(c) After a successful field goal (6-1-1-a).

If a kicker obviously attempts to kick a ball short and the ball never goes 20 yards, it is defined as an onside kick (this also applies to a safety kick).

Section 18 LINE OF SCRIMMAGE

Article 1   The Line of Scrimmage is the yard line (plane) passing through the forward point of the ball after it has been made ready for play. The term *scrimmage line,* or *line,* implies a play from scrimmage.

Article 2   A Player of Team A is on his line:

(a) when his shoulders face Team B's goal line, and

(b) if he is the snapper, no part of his body is beyond the line at the snap,

(c) <u>if he is a non-snapper, his helmet must break the vertical plane that passes through the beltline of the snapper.</u>

Note: Interlocking legs are permissible.

A.R. 3.8 Offensive A1 assumes a three-point stance with his shoulders facing defensive B's goal line. One hand is on the ground and it is on or not more than one foot behind his line. Neither of his feet nor the other hand is within one foot of his line.
Ruling: A1 is legally on his line.

Article 3   The ball has crossed the scrimmage line *(crosses line)* when, during a play from scrimmage, it has been run, fumbled, passed, or legally kicked by a Team A player, through the plane of the line and has then touched the ground or any one beyond the line.

Section 19   **NEUTRAL ZONE, START OF NEUTRAL ZONE, AND ENCROACHING**

The Neutral Zone is the space between the forward and backward points of the ball (planes). It **starts** when the ball is ready for play. (See neutral zone infraction, 7-2-3.)

A player is Encroaching (7-2-3) on the neutral zone when any part of his body is in it and contact occurs prior to the snap. The official must blow his whistle immediately.

Exception: The **snapper** is not considered in the neutral zone if no part of his body is beyond the line of scrimmage at the snap (7-2-3).

Note: The Back Judge is responsible for the 40/25-second count with the start of the neutral zone (4-6-1 and 4-7-1).

Section 20 **OFFSIDE**

A player is Offside when any part of his body or his person is in the neutral zone, or is beyond the free kick line, or fair catch kick line, when the ball is put in play.

Exceptions: The *snapper* may be in the neutral zone provided he is not beyond the line (3-18-2).

The *holder* of a *placekick* for a free kick may be beyond the free kick line (6-1-3-a-1).

The *holder of a fair catch kick* may be beyond the fair catch kick line (11-4-3).

The *kicker* may be beyond the line, but his kicking foot may not be (6-1-3-a-2).

Section 21 **OUT OF BOUNDS AND INBOUNDS SPOT**

Article 1 A player or an Official is Out of Bounds when he touches:

(a) A boundary line; or

(b) Anything other than a player, an official, or a pylon on or outside a boundary line.

Article 2 The Ball is Out of Bounds when:

(a) the runner is out of bounds;

(b) while in player possession, it touches a boundary line or anything other than a player or an official on or outside such line; or

(c) a loose ball touches a boundary line or anything on or outside such line.

Article 3   The Inbounds Spot is a spot 70 feet 9 inches in from the sideline on the yard line passing through the spot where the ball or a runner is out of bounds between the goal lines.

Under certain conditions, the ball is dead in a side zone or has been placed there as the result of a penalty. See 7-3-7 and 7-5-1 to 7-5-6.

Note: Ordinarily the out-of-bounds spot is the spot where the ball crossed a sideline. However, if a ball, while still within a boundary line, is declared out of bounds because of touching anything that is out of bounds, the out-of-bounds spot is on the yard line through the spot of the ball at the instant of such touching.

A.R. 3.9 Runner A1, with his feet inbounds, touches an official who is touching a sideline.
Ruling: Inbounds.

A.R. 3.10 Runner A1, with his feet inbounds, touches any player who is touching a sideline.
Ruling: Inbounds.

A.R. 3.11 Runner A1 fumbles backwards, and the loose ball touches a defensive player B1 who is standing on sideline, and then ball rebounds into the field of play where B1 falls on it.
Ruling: Dead ball and out of bounds as soon as the loose ball touches the player on sideline. Offensive team's ball at inbounds spot. Start game clock on the ready.

A.R. 3.12 Runner A1 touches the defensive team's pylon with any part of his body.
Ruling: Not out of bounds. The runner is not out of bounds until he touches anything other than a player or a pylon on or outside the boundary. Position of the ball

---

is determined by its position when the runner touches out of bounds.

Section 22 PASS AND PASSER

Article 1   A Pass is the movement of the ball caused by the runner who throws, shoves (shovel pass), or pushes (push pass) the ball (3-28-1).

Note: The term is also used to designate the action of a player who causes a pass as in, "He will pass the ball."

Article 2   It is a Forward Pass if:

(a) the ball initially moves forward (to a point nearer the opponent's goal line) after leaving the passer's hands; or

(b) the ball first strikes the ground, a player, an official, or anything else at a point that is nearer the opponent's goal line than the point at which the ball leaves the passer's hand.

Note 1: When a Team A player is holding the ball to pass it forward, any intentional movement forward of his hand starts a forward pass. If a Team B player contacts the passer or the ball after forward movement begins, and the ball leaves the passer's hand, a forward pass is ruled, regardless of where the ball strikes the ground or a player.

Note 2: When a Team A player is holding the ball to pass it forward, any intentional forward movement of his hand starts a forward pass, even if the player loses possession of the ball as he is attempting to tuck it back toward his body. Also, if the player has tucked the ball into his body and then loses possession, it is a fumble.

Note 3: If the player loses possession of the ball while attempting to recock his arm, it is a fumble.

Note 4: A fumble or muff going forward is disregarded as to its direction, unless the act is ruled intentional. In such cases, the fumble is a forward pass (8-1-1) and the muff is a bat (12-1-8).

A.R. 3.13 A pass legally handed forward to an eligible pass receiver is followed by a forward pass in flight from behind the line.

Ruling: A legal pass because the first handoff is not considered a forward pass.

A.R. 3.14 A pass is legally handed forward to an eligible pass receiver, who muffs the ball and it is recovered by the defensive team.

Ruling: Not an incomplete pass. It is treated as a fumble and the defensive team keeps the ball.

Article 3   A player who makes a legal forward pass is known as the Passer until the pass ends. The teammates of any player who passes forward (legally or illegally) are known collectively as the Passing Team or Passers.

Article 4   A Backward Pass (8-7-1) is any pass that is not a forward pass.

■ **Supplemental Notes**

(1) Forward, Beyond, or In Advance Of are terms that designate a point nearer the goal line of the defense unless the defense is specifically named. Converse terms are Backward or Behind.

(2) A pass parallel to a yard line or an offensive player moving parallel to it at the snap is considered backward.

(3) If a pass is batted, muffed, punched, or kicked in any direction, it does not change its original designation.

However, such an act may change the impetus (3-15-3) if sent in touch or may be a foul (12-1-8, 12-1-9).

A.R. 3.15 The ball, moving backwards in the hands of an offensive player A1, is possessed by offensive player A2 who is in advance of A1.
Ruling: Illegal forward handling unless A2 is behind his line and is eligible to receive a forward pass.

A.R. 3.16 The ball moving forward in the hands of offensive player A1, is possessed by A2 who is behind A1.
Ruling: A backward pass.

Section 23 PLACEKICK

A Placekick is a kick made by a kicker while the ball is in a fixed position on the ground except as provided for a permissible manufactured tee at kickoff (6-1-1-Note). The ball may be held in position by a teammate. See 11-4-4.

Section 24 POCKET AREA

The Pocket Area applies from the normal tackle position on each side of the center and extends backwards to the offensive team's own end line.

Section 25 POST-POSSESSION FOUL

A foul by the receiving team that occurs after a ball is legally kicked from scrimmage prior to possession changing. The ball must cross the line of scrimmage and the receiving team must retain possession of the kicked ball. See 9-5-1-Exc. 3.

Section **26** **PUNT**

A Punt is a kick made by a kicker who drops the ball
and kicks it while it is in flight (9-1-1).

Section **27** **RUNNER AND RUNNING PLAY**

Article 1   The Runner is the offensive player who is in possession
of a live ball (3-2-1), i.e., holding the ball or carrying it
in any direction.

Article 2   A Running Play is a play during which there is a runner
and which is not followed by a kick or forward pass from
behind the scrimmage line. There may be more than one
such play during the same down (14-1-12).

■ **Supplemental Notes**

(1) The exception to a running play is significant only
when a foul occurs while there is a runner prior to a
kick or pass from behind the line (8-6-1, 9-5-1, and
14-1-12).

(2) The statement, a player may advance, means that
he may become a runner, make a legal kick (9-1-1),
make a backward pass (8-7-1), or during a play
from scrimmage, an offensive player may throw a
forward pass (8-1-1) from behind his scrimmage
line, provided it is the first such pass during the
down and the ball had not been beyond the line of
scrimmage previously.

A.R. 3.17 Receiving team player B1 catches a kickoff,
advances, and fumbles. Kicking team player A2 recovers
and advances.
Ruling: While runners B1 and A2 were in possession,
there were two running plays during the same down.

Section 28 **SAFETY**

A Safety is the situation in which the ball is dead on or behind a team's own goal line provided:

(a) the impetus (3-15-3) came from a player of that team;

(b) it is not a touchdown (11-2).

Note: It is not a safety if a defensive player in the field of play intercepts a pass; catches or recovers a fumble, backward pass, scrimmage kick, free kick, or fair catch kick and his original momentum carries him into his end zone where the ball is declared dead in his team's possession. Instead the ball belongs to the defensive team at the spot where the ball was intercepted, caught or recovered (11-5-1 Exc. 2).

Section 29 **SCRIMMAGE, PLAY FROM SCRIMMAGE**

A Scrimmage Down is one that starts with a snap (3-32). From Scrimmage refers to any action from the start of the snap until the down ends or if Team A loses possession and Team B secures possession. Any subsequent action during the down, after a change of team possession, is **Not From Scrimmage.**

Note: The term scrimmage line *or* line *implies a play by A* from scrimmage. Line *is used extensively for brevity and is not to be confused with side, end, or yard line.* Line *is also used for free kick line or fair catch kick line. For given reasons, action during a free kick down (6-1), or fair catch kick down, is sometimes referred to as a play not from scrimmage.*

Section 30 **SHIFT**

A Shift is the action of two or more offensive players who (prior to a snap), after having assumed a set position, simultaneously change the position of their feet by

pivoting to or assuming a new set position with either
one foot or both feet (7-2-7).

Section 31 SNAP AND THE SNAPPER

A Snap is a backward pass that puts the ball in play to
start a scrimmage down. The Snapper is the offensive
player who attempts a snap. See 7-3-3, for conditions
pertaining to a legal snap.

Section 32 SUPPLEMENTAL NOTES (S.N.)

Supplemental Notes (S.N.) are descriptive paragraphs
used to amplify a given rule, which would otherwise be
too cumbersome or involved in its scope or wording.

An Approved Ruling (A.R.) is often used for the same
purpose (3-1). Additional Approved Rulings are also found
in *The Official Casebook of the National Football League.*

Notes are usually more specific and apply to a particular
situation. They are also used to indicate pertinent refer-
ences to other rules.

Section 33 SUSPENDED PLAYER

A Suspended Player is one who must be withdrawn, for at
least one down, for correction of illegal equipment (5-4).

Section 34 TACKLING

Tackling is the use of hands or arms by a defensive
player in his attempt to hold a runner or throw him to
the ground (12-1-6).

Section 35 TEAM A AND B, OFFENSE AND DEFENSE

Article 1   Whenever a team is in possession (3-2-7), it is the
Offense and, at such time, its opponent is the Defense.

Article 2   The team that puts the ball in play is Team A, and its opponent is Team B. For brevity, a player of Team A is referred to as A1 and his teammates as A2, A3, etc. Opponents are B1, B2, etc.

Note: A team becomes Team A when it has been designated to put ball in play, and it remains Team A until a down ends, even though there might be one or more changes of possession during the down. This is in contrast with the terms Offense *and* Defense. *Team A is always the offense when a down starts, but becomes the defense if and when B secures possession during the down, and vice versa for each change of possession.*

Article 3   A change of possession occurs when a player of the defensive team secures possession of a ball that has been kicked, passed, or fumbled by a player of the offensive team, or when the ball is awarded to the offensive team, or when the ball is awarded to the opposing team by rule. A change of possession includes but is not limited to:

(a) an interception of a forward pass; or

(b) a catch or recovery of a fumble or backward pass; or

(c) a catch or recovery of a Scrimmage Kick, Free Kick, or Fair Catch Kick.

(d) when the offensive team fails to reach the line to gain on fourth down.

(e) when the offensive team misses a field-goal attempt,

Section 36   TIMEOUT OR TIME IN

Article 1   A Time Out is an interval during which the Game Clock is stopped (4-4) and includes the intermissions (4-1-2 and 4-1-3).

Note: The term Time Out *(general) is not to be confused with a charged team time out, which is specific.* (4-5-1).

Article 2   Time In is the converse (4-3) and is also used to indicate when the clock operator is to start his clock.

Section 37   TOUCHBACK

A Touchback is the situation in which a ball is dead on or behind a team's own goal line, provided the impetus came from an opponent and provided it is not a touchdown (11-6).

Section 38   TOUCHDOWN

A Touchdown is the situation in which any part of the ball, legally in possession of a player inbounds, is on, above, or behind the opponent's goal line (plane), provided it is not a touchback (11-2).

Section 39   TRIPPING

Tripping is the use of the leg or foot in obstructing any opponent (including a runner) below the knee (12-1-5 c).

Section 40   TRY

A Try is an opportunity given a team that has just scored a touchdown to score an additional one or two points during one scrimmage down (11-3).

Section 41   YARD LINE, OWN GOAL

Article 1   A team's Own Goal during any given period is the one it is guarding. The adjacent goal line is known as its (own) goal line.

Article 2   A Yard Line is any line and its vertical plane parallel to the end line. The Yard Lines (marked or unmarked) in

---

the field of play are named by number in yards from a team's goal line to the center of the field.

Note: The yard line 19 yards from team A's goal line is called A's 19-yard line. The yard line 51 yards from A's goal line is called B's 49-yard line. (For brevity, these are referred to as A's 19 and B's 49.)

Game Timing

Rule 4

Game Timing

Section 1   **PERIODS, INTERMISSIONS, HALFTIME**

Article 1   The length of the game is 60 minutes, divided into four
               periods of 15 minutes each. In the event the score is tied
               at the end of four periods, the game is extended by an
               overtime period(s) as prescribed in Rule 16.

Article 2   There will be intervals of at least two minutes between
               the first and second periods (first half) and between the
               third and fourth periods (second half). During these
               intermissions all playing rules continue in force, and no
               representative of either team shall enter the field unless
               he is an incoming substitute, or a team attendant or
               trainer, entering to see to the welfare of a player.

**Penalty: For illegally entering the field: Loss of 15
yards from the succeeding spot (13-1-6-Pen.).**

The Back Judge times the two-minute intermissions and
shall sound his whistle (and signal visibly) after one
minute and 50 seconds. The Referee shall sound his
whistle immediately thereafter for play to start and for
the play clock operator to start the 25-second clock. See
4-6-2.

Article 3   Between the second and third periods, there shall be an
               intermission of 12 minutes, plus any prescribed delay
               times established by the League office for teams to return
               to their locker rooms. During this intermission, play is
               suspended, and teams may leave the field. The Back
               Judge will time halftime. See 13-1-1 for fouls by non-
               players between halves.

Article 4   The stadium electric clock shall be the official time. The
               game clock operator shall start and stop the clock upon

the signal of any official in accordance with the rules. The Line Judge (15-5-2) shall supervise timing of the game, and in case the stadium clock becomes inoperative, or if it is not being operated correctly, he shall take over official timing on the field.

Note: Game officials can correct the game clock only before the next legal snap or kick, including an untimed down or try.

Section 2 **STARTING A PERIOD OR HALF**

Article 1 Both teams must be on the field to kick off at the scheduled time for the start of each half. Prior to the start of the game, both teams are required to appear on the field at least 10 minutes prior to the scheduled kickoff in order to ensure sufficient time for proper warmup. Designated members of the officiating crew must notify both head coaches personally of the scheduled time for kickoff prior to the start of each half.

Penalties:

(a) **For delaying the start of a half: Loss of 15 yards from the spot of the kickoff as determined by 6-1-2-a.**

(b) **For failure to appear on the field at least 10 minutes prior to the scheduled kickoff: Loss of the coin-toss option for both halves and overtime, and loss of 15 yards from the spot of the kickoff.**

Article 2 Not more than three minutes before the kickoff of the first half, the Referee, in the presence of both team's captains (limit of six per team, all of whom must be uniformed members of the Active List) shall toss a coin at the center of the field. Prior to the Referee's toss, the call of "heads" or "tails" must be made by the captain of the visiting team, or by the captain designated by the

---

Referee if there is no home team. Unless the winner of the toss defers his choice to the second half, he must choose one of two privileges, and the loser is given the other. The two privileges are:

(a) The opportunity to receive the kickoff; or

(b) The choice of goal his team will defend.

 Penalty: For failure to comply: Loss of coin-toss option for both halves and overtime, and loss of 15 yards from the spot of the kickoff for the first half only.

For the second half, the captain who lost the pregame toss is to have the first choice of the two privileges listed in (a) or (b), unless one of the teams lost its first and second half options pursuant to 4-2-1, or unless the winner of the pregame toss deferred his choice to the second half, in which case he must choose (a) or (b) above. Immediately prior to the start of the second half, the captains of both teams must inform the Referee of their respective choices.

A captain's first choice from any alternative privileges listed above is final and not subject to change.

Article 3 At the end of the first and third periods, the teams must change goals. Team possession, the number of the succeeding down, the relative position of the ball on the field of play, and the line to gain remain the same.

Section 3 **STARTING THE GAME CLOCK**

Article 1 The game clock operator shall start the game clock (time in) after a free kick when the ball is legally touched in the field of play. The game clock shall not start if:

(a) the receiving team recovers the ball in the end zone and does not carry the ball into the field of play;

(b) the kicking team recovers the ball in the field of play; or

(c) the receiving team signals for and makes a fair catch.

A.R. 4.1 a) With three seconds remaining in the second quarter, A1 attempts an onside kick from the A30. The kick is caught or recovered legally at the A41: a) by A2, b) by B1 who signals for and completes a fair catch, c) by B1 on his feet and he immediately goes to the ground, or d) by B1 on the ground and he makes no effort to get up or advance.

Rulings:

a) A's ball, first-and-10 on A41. Three seconds on the clock. (No time runs off the clock).

b) B's ball, first-and-10 on A41. Three seconds on the clock. (No time runs off the clock).

c) B's ball, first-and-10 on A41. Two seconds on the clock. (One second runs off the clock).

d) B's ball, first-and-10 on A41. Two seconds on the clock. (One second runs off the clock).

A.R. 4.1 b) During the last two minutes of the game the offensive team safety kicks from the A20.
Ruling: Time in starts when the safety kick is legally touched by any player in the field of play.

Note: No extension of the automatic timeouts in this section shall be allowed unless any player requests a team timeout, or a Referee orders a team timeout or suspends play himself.

Article 2   Following any timeout (3-37), the game clock shall be started on a scrimmage down when the ball is next snapped, except in the following situations:

(a) Whenever a runner goes out of bounds on a play from scrimmage, the game clock is started when an official spots the ball at the inbounds spot, and the

Referee gives the signal to start the game clock,
except that the clock will start on the snap:

(1) after a change of possession;

(2) after the two-minute warning of the first half; or

(3) inside the last five minutes of the second half.

A.R. 4.2 With three minutes remaining in the first
quarter, back A2 takes a handoff and runs out of bounds
at the A27.
Ruling: Stop game clock. Time in on Referee's signal.

A.R. 4.3 B7 intercepts a forward pass and runs out of
bounds at the A14.
Ruling: Stop game clock. Time in on snap.

(b) If the player who originally takes the snap is tackled
behind the line of scrimmage prior to the two-minute
warning, the game clock starts when the Referee
signals that the ball is ready for play. (The play clock
starts at 40 seconds immediately after the tackle.)

(c) If there is an injury timeout prior to the two-minute
warning, the game clock is started as if the injury
timeout had not occurred.

(d) If there is an excess team timeout after the two-
minute warning, the game clock is started as if the
excess timeout had not occurred.

(e) If there is a Referee's timeout, the game clock is
started as if the Referee's timeout had not occurred.

(f) If the game clock is stopped after a down in which
there was a foul by either team, following enforcement or declination of a penalty, the game clock will
start as if the foul had not occurred, except that the
clock will start on the snap:

(1) if the foul occurs after the two-minute warning of the first half;

(2) if the foul occurs inside the last five minutes of the second half; or

(3) if a specific rule prescribes otherwise.

A.R. 4.4 Second–and-10 on A30. Runner A1 goes to the A40 and where he is tackled. During A1's run, A2 clipped B1 at the A35.
Ruling: A's ball second-and-20 on A20. Game Clock starts on ready-to-play signal after penalty is enforced except inside the last two minutes of the first half or the last five minutes of the second half.

A.R. 4.5 Second-and-10 on A30. Runner A1 goes to the A40 and steps out of bounds there. During A1's run, A2 clipped B1 at the A35.
Ruling: A's ball second-and-20 on A20. Game clock starts with Referee's ready signal as ball was dead when runner ran out of bounds, except inside the last two minutes of first half or inside last five minutes of the second half.

(g) If a fumble or backward pass by any player goes out of bounds, the game clock starts when an official places the ball at the inbounds line, and the Referee signals that the ball is ready for play.

(h) When there is a 10-second runoff, the game clock starts when the Referee signals that the ball is ready for play.

(i) <u>During the Try, which is an untimed down,</u>

(j) When a specific rule prescribes otherwise.

Article 3   The game clock operator shall start the game clock for a fair-catch kick down when the ball is kicked.

Section 4   **STOPPING THE GAME CLOCK**

The game clock operator shall stop the game clock (timeout) upon a signal by any official or upon his own positive knowledge:

(a) at the end of a down in which there is a free kick or fair-catch kick;

(b) when the kicking team recovers a scrimmage kick that has been touched by the receiving team beyond the line of scrimmage;

(c) when the ball is out of bounds;

(d) when the ball is dead on or behind a goal line;

(e) at the end of a down during which a foul occurs;

(f) when a forward pass is incomplete;

(g) when the player who originally takes the snap is tackled behind the line of scrimmage;

Exception: After the two-minute warning of a half, the game clock shall not be stopped.

A.R. 4.6 Quarterback A1 drops back to pass and is tackled behind the line.
Ruling: Stop the game clock until the ball can be respotted at succeeding spot. (40-second play clock starts when timeout signal is given).

(h) at the time of a foul for which the ball remains dead or is dead immediately;

(i) when the Referee signals the two-minute warning for a half;

(j) when a down is completed during which or after there is a change of possession; or

(k) when any official signals a timeout for any other reason.

Section 5 TIMEOUTS

Article 1 The Referee shall suspend play while the ball is dead and declare a charged team timeout upon the request for a timeout by the head coach or any player to any official.

Item 1: Three Timeouts Allowed. A team is allowed three charged team timeouts during each half.

Item 2: Length of Timeouts. Charged team timeouts shall be two minutes in length, unless the timeout is not used by television for a commercial break. Timeouts shall be 30 seconds in length when the designated number of television commercials have been exhausted in a quarter, if it is a second charged team timeout in the same dead-ball period, or when the Referee so indicates.

Item 3: Consecutive Team Timeouts. Each team may be granted a charged team timeout during the same dead-ball period, but a second charged team timeout by either team during the same dead-ball period is prohibited. Such team timeouts may follow a Referee's timeout or any automatic timeouts in Section 4 above.

Item 4: Unsportsmanlike Conduct. An attempt to call an excess team timeout or to call a second timeout in the same dead-ball period by Team B in an attempt to "freeze" a kicker, will be considered unsportsmanlike conduct and will subject the offending team to a 15-yard penalty (See 12-3). This will apply to field goal or Try attempts.

Note: If an attempt is made to call a timeout in such situations, the officials shall not grant a timeout; instead, play will continue, and a penalty will be called, with customary enforcement. *If a timeout is inadvertently granted, the penalty shall also be enforced.* See 12-3-1-v.

Article 2 If an official determines a player to be injured, or if attendants from the bench come on the field to assist an injured player, an injury timeout will be called by the Referee.

A.R. 4.7 Runner A1 is tackled and appears injured since he does not move.
Ruling: Official should call timeout for injured player. Official should not try to determine if player is injured. Timeout is not charged if conditions are not violated.

Article 3 When an injury timeout is called, the injured player must leave the game for the completion of one down. The player will be permitted to remain in the game if:

(a) either team calls a charged team timeout;

(b) the injury is the result of a foul by an opponent; or

(c) the period ends or the two-minute warning occurs before the next snap.

At the conclusion of an injury timeout, the game clock will start as if the injury timeout had not occurred. If either team takes, or is charged with, a timeout, the clock will start on the snap.

Article 4 After the two-minute warning of a half, the following shall apply:

(a) If a team has not used its three charged team timeouts, the team of the injured player will be charged a team timeout, unless:

(i) the injury is the result of a foul by an opponent;

(ii) the injury occurs during a down in which there is a change of possession, a successful field goal, or an attempted Try; or

(iii) the opponent calls a timeout.

(b) If a team has used its three charged team timeouts, an excess team timeout shall be called by the
Referee, unless:

(i) the injury is the result of a foul by an opponent;

(ii) the injury occurs during a down in which there
is a change of possession, a successful field goal,
or an attempted Try; or

(iii) the opponent calls a timeout.

**Penalty: For the second and each subsequent excess
team timeout after the two-minute warning: Loss of five
yards from the succeeding spot for delay of the game.**

c) The player must leave the game for the completion
of one down, unless:

(i) the injury is the result of a foul by an opponent;
or

(ii) either team calls a charged team timeout.

d) No yardage penalty will be assessed for the first
excess team timeout, but a 10-second runoff of the
game clock may be applicable pursuant to (f) below.
At the conclusion of an excess timeout taken while
time is in, the game clock shall start with the ready-
for-play signal. For any excess timeout charged to the
defense, the play clock is reset to 40 seconds.

e) If the Referee has already called an excess team
timeout in that half for a team, any subsequent
excess timeout for that team will result in a five-yard
penalty. (Such penalty shall be considered a foul
between downs and will not offset a foul by the
defense or be part of a multiple foul by the offense.)

f) If an excess team timeout is charged against a team in
possession of the ball, and time is in when the excess
timeout is called, the ball shall not be put in play
until the time on the game clock has been reduced
by 10 seconds, if the defense so chooses.

A.R. 4.8   Offensive team A, in the last two minutes of the half and the clock running:

a) Requests its fourth timeout because of an injured player.

Ruling: Granted. No five-yard penalty. Player has to be removed. Ten-second runoff. Ball will not be put in play until the Referee blows his whistle and gives the wind-the-clock signal.

b) Requests its fifth timeout because of an injured player.

Ruling: Granted. Five-yard penalty. Player has to be removed. Ten-second runoff. Ball will not be put in play until the Referee blows his whistle and gives the wind-the-clock signal.

■ Supplemental Notes

(1) Either half can end as the result of the 10-second runoff referenced in (f) above.

(2) If an injury timeout is called for both teams during or after a down, charged team timeouts and/or excess team timeouts are charged as appropriate, but no yardage or 10-second runoff penalties shall be enforced.

(3) If a foul by either team occurs during a down in which there is also an injury, such foul does not affect the charging of an excess timeout, but it does prevent a 10-second runoff that may result from the excess timeout, because the foul stopped the clock.

(4) The Rules Committee deprecates feigning injuries, with subsequent withdrawal, to obtain a timeout without penalty. Coaches are urged to cooperate in discouraging this practice.

(5) There can never be a 10-second runoff against the defensive team.

(6) See Rule 16 (Sudden-Death Procedures), Section 1, Articles 3, 5, and 6 for application to overtime games.

Article 5   Provided that calling timeout is not in conflict with another rule, the Referee may suspend play and stop the clock (Referee's timeout) at any time without penalty to either team when playing time is being consumed because of an unintentional delay. Such situations include but are not limited to the following:

(a) when there is the possibility of a measurement for a first down, or if the Referee is consulting with a captain about one;

(b) when there is an undue pileup on the runner, or while determining possession after a fumble while time is in;

(c) when there is an undue delay by officials in spotting the ball for the next snap;

(d) if the snap is made before the officials can assume their positions. See 4-6-5 b if it is a repeated act;

(e) when there is an injury to an official or member of the chain crew;

(f) during an officials' conference (see 15-1-6); or

(g) while repairing or replacing game equipment, except player equipment.

After a Referee's timeout, the game clock will start pursuant to Rule 4, Section 3, as if the Referee's timeout had not occurred.

Section 6 **DELAY OF GAME**

Article 1 It is a delay of the game if the ball is not put into play by a snap within 40 seconds after the start of the play clock. The play clock operator shall time the interval between plays upon signals from game officials. The 40-second interval starts when a play ends, unless Article 2 below applies.

Article 2 In the event of certain administrative stoppages or other delays, a team will have 25 seconds, beginning with the Referee's whistle, to put the ball in play by a snap or a kick. Such stoppages include, but are not limited to, the following:

(a) a change of possession;

(b) a charged team timeout;

(c) the two-minute warning;

(d) the expiration of a period;

(e) a penalty enforcement;

(f) a Try; or

(g) a Free Kick.

A 25-second interval will be used in these situations, even if the 40-second clock is already counting down.

Article 3 If the play clock is stopped prior to the snap for any reason, after the stoppage has concluded, the time remaining on the play clock shall be the same as when it stopped, unless:

(a) the stoppage has been for a charged team timeout, the two-minute warning, the expiration of a period, a penalty enforcement, or an Instant Replay challenge prior to the two-minute warning, in which case the play clock shall be reset to 25 seconds;

(b) the stoppage has been for an Instant Replay review after the two-minute warning that results in a reversal, in which case the play clock shall be reset to 25 seconds;

(c) the stoppage has been for an excess timeout while time is in that is charged to the defense, in which case the play clock shall be reset to 40 seconds; or

(d) fewer than 10 seconds remain on the play clock, in which case it shall be reset to 10 seconds.

Article 4 If the ball is not put in play within the applicable period, the Back Judge shall blow his whistle for the foul, and the ball remains dead. See 14-6-Exc. 4.

Article 5 Other examples of action or inaction that are to be construed as delay of the game include, but are not limited to, the following:

(a) a player unnecessarily remains on a dead ball or on a runner who has been downed;

(b) the snapper repeatedly snaps the ball after the neutral zone is established and before the Referee can assume his position (see 7-3-3-c-2);

(c) undue delay by either team in assembling after a timeout;

(d) a defensive player aligned in a stationary position within one yard of the line of scrimmage makes quick and abrupt actions that are not a part of normal defensive player movement and are an obvious attempt to cause an offensive player(s) to foul (false start). (The Referee shall blow his whistle immediately.);

(e) spiking or throwing the ball in the field of play after a down has ended, except after a score;

Penalty: For delay of the game: Loss of five yards:

(a) **from the succeeding spot if it occurs between downs. The ball remains dead; or**

(b) **from the previous spot if the ball was in play.**

Section 7   **ACTIONS TO CONSERVE TIME**

Article 1   A team is not permitted to conserve time inside of one
minute of either half by committing any of the following
acts:

(a) a foul by either team that prevents the snap (i.e., false
start, encroachment, etc.)

(b) intentional grounding;

(c) an illegal forward pass thrown from beyond the line
of scrimmage;

(d) throwing a backward pass out of bounds;

(e) spiking or throwing the ball in the field of play after
a down has ended, except after a touchdown; or

(f) any other intentional foul that causes the clock to
stop.

**Penalty: For Illegally Conserving Time: Loss of five
yards unless a larger distance penalty is applicable.**

**When actions referred to above are committed by the
offensive team while time is in, officials will run 10
seconds off the game clock before permitting the ball
to be put in play on the ready-for-play signal. The
game clock will start on the ready-for-play signal. If the
offensive team has timeouts remaining, it will have the
option of using a timeout in lieu of a 10-second runoff,
in which case the game clock will start on the snap
after the timeout. The defense always has the option to
decline the 10-second runoff and have the yardage
penalty enforced, but if the yardage penalty is declined,
the 10-second runoff is also declined.**

**If the action is by the defense, the play clock will be
reset to 40 seconds, and the game clock will start on**

the ready signal, unless the offense chooses to have the clock start on the snap. If the defense has timeouts remaining, it will have the option of using a timeout in lieu of the game clock being started.

A.R. 4.9 With eight seconds remaining in the first half, A1 throws a backward pass out-of-bounds to stop the game clock.
Ruling: Half over, 10-second runoff for conserving time.

A.R. 4.10 With seven seconds remaining in the first half, guard A1 commits a false start in order to stop the game clock.
Ruling: Half over, 10-second runoff for conserving time.

Note 1: More than two successive delay penalties during the same down, after a warning, is unsportsmanlike conduct (12-3-1-n).

Note 2: Certain acts of delay may involve stopping the game clock immediately. Repeated violations of the substitution rule to conserve time are unsportsmanlike conduct (12-3-1-m and 5-2-2).

Article 2   Inside one minute of either half, if there is a violation of the substitution rule while the ball is dead and time is in, in addition to the applicable yardage penalty for illegal substitution, there will be a 10-second runoff pursuant to Article 1 above.

 Penalty: For Illegal Substitution: Loss of five yards (unless a larger distance penalty is applicable) and a 10-second runoff.

Article 3   In the last 40 seconds of either half, if there is a defensive foul prior to the snap while time is in, the half will end, unless the defense has timeouts remaining, or the offense chooses to have the Game Clock start on the snap.

Article 4   If a replay review inside of one minute of either half results in the on-field ruling being reversed and the correct ruling would not have stopped the game clock, then the officials will run 10 seconds off the game clock before permitting the ball to be put in play on the ready-for-play signal. All normal rules regarding 10-second runoffs will apply.

Section 8   EXTENSION OF A PERIOD OR A HALF

Article 1   If time expires at the end of any period while the ball is in play, the period continues until the down ends.

Article 2   At the election of the opponent, a period may be extended for one untimed down, if any of the following occurs during a down during which time in the period expires:

(a) If there is a foul by the defensive team that is accepted, the offensive team may choose to extend the period by an untimed down after enforcement of the penalty. If the first or third period is not so extended, any accepted penalty is enforced before the start of the succeeding period.

(b) If there is a foul by the offense, there shall be no extension of the period. If the foul occurs on the last play of the half, a score by the offense is not counted. However, the period may be extended for an untimed down, upon the request of the defense, if the offensive team's foul is for:
    (1) illegal touching of a kick;
    (2) fair-catch interference;
    (3) a palpably unfair act;
    (4) a personal foul or unsportsmanlike conduct foul committed prior to an interception of a forward pass or the recovery of a backward pass or fumble; or

(5) a foul by the kicking team prior to a player of the receiving team securing possession of the ball during a down in which there is a safety kick, a scrimmage kick, or a free kick.

A.R. 4.11 Fourth-and-10 on B40. On the last play of the first quarter, offensive team misses an attempted field goal. Defensive team was offside. There is a strong wind at their back.
Ruling: Offensive team has option of extending period by an untimed down. It can put ball in play from the B35 and kick the same way. If the period is not extended, it would be fourth and five on the B35 at start of second period.

A.R. 4.12 Third-and-10 on A45. Offensive team is offside. Quarterback A1 throws a legal pass which is completed to end A2 who runs for a score. Time for second half expired during play.
Ruling: No score and game over as it was an offensive foul on last play of half.

A.R. 4.13 Fourth-and-10 on A20. A punt is touched illegally by kicking team player A1 on the A45 who falls on the ball as time runs out in second half.
Ruling: One scrimmage down allowed, if desired, by receivers from the A45. Untimed down as it was an illegal touch.

(c) If a double foul occurs during the last down of either half, the period shall be extended by an untimed down.

Exceptions: The half is not extended if:

(1) both fouls are dead-ball fouls;

(2) if there is a major-minor double foul ("5 vs. 15"), and the major foul is by the offense (see 14-3-1-Exc.); or

(3) if there is a double foul with a change of possession ("clean hands" rule, see 14-3-2) that does not involve a replay of the down.

(If a double foul occurs on the last play of the first or third periods, the period is not extended.)

A.R. 4.14 Defensive B1 intercepts at midfield on the last play of either half. On runback, B2 clips at the A40. A1 piles on after runner B1 is tackled on the A30.
Ruling: Extend the period with an untimed down from A40. B's ball. See 14-3-3.

(d) If a touchdown is made on the last play of a period, the Try attempt shall be made (except during a sudden-death period).

(e) If no fair-catch signal is given and the kickers interfere with the receiver's opportunity to catch a kick, the receiving team may extend the period by a down from scrimmage.

(f) If a fair-catch is signaled and made, the receivers may choose to extend the period by a fair-catch kick down (10-2-4). If the first or third period is not so extended, the receivers may start the succeeding period with a snap or fair-catch kick (11-4-3).

A.R. 4.15 The offensive team punts as time for the half expires. Defensive player B1 gives a valid fair-catch signal and catches the ball on the A35.
Ruling: The receiving team may extend the period by a fair-catch kick (10-2-4, 11-4-3).

(g) If a fair catch is signaled and the kickers interfere with a receiver's opportunity to catch a kick, the receiving team may extend the period by either a down from scrimmage or a fair-catch kick (10-2-4).

(h) If a safety results from a foul during the last play of a half, the score counts. A safety kick is made if requested by the receivers.

If the first or third period is extended for any reason, or if a touchdown occurs during the last play of such a period, any additional play, including a Try attempt, shall be completed before the teams change goals.

If any period is extended for any reason, it shall continue until the completion of a down free from any foul specified in (a) through (i) above.

Players,
Substitutes,
Equipment,
General Rules

Rule 5

Players, Substitutes, Equipment, General Rules

Section 1   **PLAYERS**

Article 1   The game is played by two teams of 11 players each. If a snap, free kick, or fair-catch kick is made while a team has fewer than 11 players on the field of play or the end zone, the ball is in play, and there is no penalty. If a team has more than 11 players on the field of play or the end zone when a snap, free kick, or fair-catch kick is made, the ball is in play, and it is a foul.

Penalty: For more than 11 players on the field of play or the end zone while the ball is in play: Loss of five yards from the previous spot.

Article 2   All players must wear numerals on their jerseys in accordance with Rule 5, Section 4, Article 3(c). Such numerals must be by playing position, as follows:

(a) quarterbacks, punters, and placekickers: 1-19;

(b) running backs and defensive backs: 20-49;

(c) centers: 50-<u>79;</u>

(d) offensive guards and tackles: 60-79;

(e) wide receivers: 10-19 and 80-89;

(f) tight ends: 80-89;

(g) defensive linemen: 60-79 and 90-99; and

(h) linebackers: 50-59 and 90-99.

<u>If a player changes his position during his playing career in the NFL, and such change moves him from a position as an ineligible pass receiver to that of an eligible pass</u>

receiver, or from a position as an eligible pass receiver to that of an ineligible pass receiver, he must be issued an appropriate new jersey numeral. A change in jersey numeral is not required if the change is from an ineligible position to another incligible position, or from an eligible position to another eligible position, provided that the player has participated at least one season at his position prior to the change.

Any request to wear a numeral for a special position not specified above (e.g., H-back) must be made to the Commissioner.

During the preseason period when playing rosters are larger, the League will allow duplication and other temporary deviations from the numbering scheme specified above, but the rule must be adhered to for all players during the regular season and postseason. Clubs must make numerals available to adhere to the rule, even if it requires returning to circulation a numeral that has been retired or withheld for other reasons. See 5-3-1 for reporting a change of position.

Section 2	**SUBSTITUTES AND WITHDRAWN PLAYERS**
Article 1	There can never be more than 11 players in the offensive huddle while the play clock is running. If there is a foul, the whistle is blown immediately, and the ball remains dead.
Article 2	A substitute becomes a player when:

    (a) he participates in at least one play (including a play negated by penalty prior to the snap or during the play); or

    (b) he is on the field of play or the end zone when a snap, fair-catch kick, or free kick is made, or when a snap, fair-catch kick, or free kick is imminent.

A player becomes a substitute when he is withdrawn from the game and does not participate in at least one play. A play negated by penalty prior to the snap or during the play counts as a missed play.

Article 3 Any number of substitutes may enter the field of play or the end zone while the ball is dead.

Article 4 If a substitute enters the field of play or the end zone while the ball is in play, it is an illegal substitution. If an illegal substitute interferes with the play, it may be a palpably unfair act (see 12-3-3).

Article 5 The following are applicable to any offensive substitute who is entering the game:

(a) He must move onto the field of play or the end zone as far as the inside of the field numerals prior to the snap to be a legal substitution. If he does not, and is on the field of play or end zone at the time of a legal snap, he is an illegal substitute.

(b) If he approaches the huddle and communicates with a teammate(s), he is required to participate in at least one play before being withdrawn. Violations of this rule may be penalized for unsportsmanlike conduct.

Note: The intent of the rule is to prevent teams from using simulated substitutions to confuse an opponent, while still permitting a player(s) to enter and leave without participating in a play in certain situations, such as a change in a coaching decision on fourth down, even though he has approached the huddle and communicated with a teammate. Similarly, if a player who participated in the previous play leaves the playing field by mistake, and returns to the playing field prior to the snap, he is not required to reach the inside of the field numerals, provided that the defense has the opportunity to match up with him. However, a substitute (i.e., someone who did not participate in the previous play) is required to reach the inside of the field numerals.

Article 6   A player or players who have been replaced must leave the playing field or end zone on their own team's side between the end lines prior to the next snap, free kick, or fair-catch kick.

Article 7   A player must be withdrawn and substituted for when he is disqualified (see 12-2, 12-3) or suspended (see 5-4). A suspended player may re-enter after at least one legal snap, provided that the reason for his suspension has been corrected. A disqualified player must leave the playing field enclosure and go to the team locker room within a reasonable time.

Article 8   Penalties for illegal substitution or withdrawal are:

(a) For 12 or more players in the offensive huddle (whistle blown immediately and ball remains dead): Loss of five yards from the succeeding spot.

(b) For a substitute entering the field during a live ball: Loss of five yards.

(c) For interference with the play by a substitute who enters the field during a live ball: Palpably unfair act (see 12-3-3).

(d) For an offensive substitute who does not move onto the field as far as the inside of the field numerals: Loss of five yards from the previous spot.

(e) For an offensive substitute who moves onto the field inside the field numerals and leaves without participating in one play: Unsportsmanlike Conduct.

(f) For a withdrawn player on the field at the snap, free kick, or fair-catch kick: Loss of five yards from the previous spot.

(g) For a withdrawn player clearing the field on the opponents' side or across an end line: Loss of five yards from the previous spot.

(h) For illegal return of a suspended player: Loss of five yards from the previous spot if discovery is made while the ball is in play, or five yards from the succeeding spot if discovered between downs, in which case the ball remains dead.

(i) For return of a disqualified player: Loss of 15 yards from the previous spot if discovery is made while the ball is in play, or 15 yards from the succeeding spot if discovered between downs, in which case the ball remains dead, and, in either case, exclusion from the playing field enclosure.

■ Supplemental Note

If the illegal return of a player is not discovered until the end of a down, but prior to the start of the next one, enforcement is from the previous spot when definitely known. Otherwise, enforcement is from the succeeding spot as a foul between downs (see 14-5).

Article 9   Following a timeout or change of possession, the ball will not be declared ready for play until the offense has brought 11 players into its huddle inside the inbounds lines (hashmarks). If the offensive team refuses to leave the sideline prior to the ball being declared ready for play, it will be warned once. Thereafter, the offense will be penalized 15 yards for unsportsmanlike conduct.

Penalty: For Unsportsmanlike Conduct after a warning: Loss of 15 yards from the succeeding spot.

If there is an offensive substitution that occurs after the offensive team has broken its huddle, the play clock will be stopped, and the defense will be allowed an opportunity to matchup.

Article 10   If a substitution is made by the offense, the offense shall not be permitted to snap the ball until the defense has been permitted to respond with its substitutions. While in the process of a substitution (or simulated substitution), the offense is prohibited from rushing quickly to the line of scrimmage and snapping the ball in an obvious attempt to cause a defensive foul (i.e., too many men on the field). If, in the judgment of the officials, this occurs, the following procedure will apply:

(a) The Umpire will stand over the ball until the Referee deems that the defense has had a reasonable time to complete its substitutions.

(b) If a play takes place and a defensive foul for too many players on the field results, no penalties will be enforced, except for personal fouls and unsportsmanlike conduct, and the down will be replayed. At this time, the Referee will notify the head coach that any further use of this tactic will result in a penalty for unsportsmanlike conduct.

Note: The quick-snap rule does not apply after the two-minute warning of either half, or if there is not a substitution by the offense

(c) On a fourth down punting situation, the Referee and the Umpire will not allow a quick snap that prevents the defense from having a reasonable time to complete its substitutions. This applies throughout the entire game.

Article 11   Using entering substitutes, legally returning players, substitutes on sidelines, or withdrawn players to confuse opponents, or lingering by players leaving the field when being replaced by a substitute, is unsportsmanlike conduct.

See 12-3-1-k. The offense is prevented from sending simulated substitutions onto the field toward its huddle and returning them to the sideline without completing the substitution in an attempt to confuse the defense.

Penalty: For Unsportsmanlike Conduct after a warning: Loss of 15 yards from the succeeding spot.

Section 3   CHANGES IN POSITION

Article 1   An offensive player wearing the number of an ineligible pass receiver (50-79 and 90-99) is permitted to line up in the position of an eligible pass receiver (1-49 and 80-89), and an offensive player wearing the number of an eligible pass receiver is permitted to line up in the position of an ineligible pass receiver, provided that he immediately reports the change in his eligibility status to the Referee, who will inform the defensive team.

He must participate in such eligible or ineligible position as long as he is continuously in the game, but prior to each play he must again report his status to the Referee, who will inform the defensive team. The game clock shall not be stopped, and the ball shall not be put in play until the Referee takes his normal position.

Article 2   A player who has reported a change in his eligibility status to the Referee is permitted to return to a position indicated by the eligibility status of his number <u>after</u>:

(a) a team timeout;

(b) the end of a quarter;

(c) the two-minute warning;

(d) a foul;

(e) a replay challenge;

(f) a touchdown;

(g) a completed kick from scrimmage;

(h) a change of possession; or

(i) if the player has been withdrawn for one legal snap.
A player withdrawn for one legal snap may re-enter
at a position indicated by the eligibility status of his
number, unless he again reports to the Referee that
he is assuming a position other than that designated
by the eligibility status of his number.

Article 3   Each offensive and defensive team is permitted to have
one player on the field with a speaker in his helmet.
There must be a visual indicator on the player's helmet
to identify him. Each player listed as a quarterback on
the pregame deactivation report and two defensive
players, designated by their teams as a primary and
backup user, are permitted to have speakers in their
helmets.

When the backup quarterback enters the game for the
first time, or re-enters the game if he has previously been
in the game and removed, he must report to the Referee.

Whenever the backup defensive user enters the game
wearing a helmet with a speaker, he must report to the
Umpire. If the primary defensive user subsequently re-
enters the game wearing a helmet with a speaker, he must
report to the Umpire.

A team may not have two players in the game at the
same time with speakers in their helmets.

**Penalty: If a player fails to notify the Referee of a
change in his status when required: Loss of five yards
for illegal substitution.**

Section 4   EQUIPMENT, UNIFORMS, PLAYER APPEARANCE

Article 1   Throughout the game-day period while in view of the
stadium and television audience, including during
pregame warm-ups, all players must dress in a profes-

sional manner under the uniform standards specified in this Section 4. They must wear equipment offering reasonable protection to themselves while reasonably avoiding risk of injury to other players. They generally must present an appearance that is appropriate to representing their individual clubs and the National Football League. The term uniform, as used in this policy, applies to every piece of equipment worn by a player, including helmet, shoulder pads, thigh pads, knee pads, and any other item of protective gear, and to every visible item of apparel, including but not limited to pants, jerseys, wristbands, gloves, stockings, shoes, visible undergarments, and accessories such as headwear, worn under helmets and hand towels. All visible items worn on game-day by players must be issued by the club or the League, or, if from outside sources, must have approval in advance by the League office.

Team Colors

Article 2   Pursuant to the official colors established for each NFL club in the League Constitution and Bylaws, playing squads are permitted to wear only those colors or a combination of those colors for helmets, jerseys, pants, and stockings; provided that white is also an available color for jerseys and mandatory color for the lower portion of stockings [see 5-3-3-(i), "Stockings," below]. Each player on a given team must wear the same colors on his uniform as all other players on his team in the same game. Before July 1 each year, home clubs are required to report to the League office their choice of jersey color (either white or official team color) for their home games of that forthcoming season and visiting clubs must wear the opposite. For preseason, regular season, or postseason games, the two competing teams may wear jerseys in their official colors (non-white), provided the Commissioner determines that such colors are of sufficient contrast.

Mandatory Equipment, Apparel

Article 3 All players must wear the equipment and uniform apparel listed below, which must be of a suitably protective nature, must be designed and produced by a professional manufacturer, and must not be cut, reduced in size, or otherwise altered unless for medical reasons approved in advance by the Commissioner. During pregame warm-ups players may omit certain protective equipment at their option, except that helmets must be worn. Where additional rules are applicable to specific categories of mandatory equipment or apparel, or where related equipment is optional, such provisions are also spelled out below.

Helmets, Face Protectors

(a) Helmet with chin strap (white only) fastened and facemask attached. Facemasks must not be more than ⅝-inch in diameter and must be made of rounded material, transparent materials are prohibited.

Clear (transparent) plastic shields are optional. Tinted eye shields may be worn only after the League office is supplied with appropriate medical documentation and approval is subsequently granted. The League office has final approval.

No visible identification of a manufacturer's name or logo on the exterior of a helmet or on any attachment to a helmet is permitted unless provided for under a commercial arrangement between the League and manufacturer; in no event is identification of any helmet manufacturer permitted on the visible surface of a rear cervical pad. All helmets must carry a small NFL shield logo on the rear lower-left exterior <u>and an approved warning label</u> on the rear lower-right exterior. <u>Both</u> labels will be supplied in quantity by the League <u>office</u>.

Jerseys

(b) Jersey must cover all pads and other protective equipment worn on the torso and upper arms, and must be appropriately tailored to remain tucked into the uniform pants throughout the game. Tearaway jerseys are prohibited. Mesh jerseys with large <u>fishnet</u> material (commonly referred to as "bullet-hole" or "port-hole" mesh) are also prohibited. Surnames of players in letters a minimum of 2½-inches high must be affixed to the exterior of jerseys across the upper back above the numerals; nicknames are prohibited. All jerseys must carry a small NFL Equipment logo at the middle of the yoke of the neck on the front of the garment. All fabrics must be approved by the League office prior to production.

Numerals

(c) Numerals on the back and front of jerseys in accordance with Rule 5, Section 1, Article <u>2</u>. Such numerals must be a minimum of 8 inches high and 4 inches wide, and their color must be in sharp contrast with the color of the jersey. Smaller numerals should be worn on the tops of the shoulders or upper arms of the jersey. Small numerals on the back of the helmet or on the uniform pants are optional.

Pants

(d) Pants must be worn over the entire knee area; pants shortened or rolled up to meet the stockings above the knee are prohibited. No part of the pants may be cut away unless an appropriate gusset or other device is used to replace the removed material. All pants must carry a small NFL Equipment logo on the front left groin area of the pants, midway between the fly opening and side seam, and ½-inch below the belt.

Shoulder Pads

(e) Shoulder pads must be completely covered by the uniform jersey.

Stockings

(f) Stockings must cover the entire area from the shoe to the bottom of the pants, and must meet the pants below the knee. Players are permitted to wear as many layers of stockings and tape on the lower leg as they prefer, provided the exterior is a one-piece stocking that includes solid white from the top of the shoe to the mid-point of the lower leg, and approved team color or colors (non-white) from that point to the top of the stocking. Uniform stockings may not be altered (e.g. over-stretched, cut at the toes, or sewn short) in order to bring the line between solid white and team colors lower or higher than the mid-point of the lower leg. No other stockings and/or opaque tape may be worn over the one-piece, two-color uniform stocking. Barefoot punters and placekickers may omit the stocking of the kicking foot in preparation for and during kicking plays.

Shoes

(g) Shoes must be of standard football design, including "sneaker" type shoes such as basketball shoes, cross-training shoes, etc. League-approved tri-colored shoes are permitted with black, white, and one team color. Each team must select a dominant color for its shoes, either black or white (with shoelace color conforming to the dominant color of the tongue area of the manufacturer's shoe). The selection of dominant color must be reported by each team to the League office no later than July 1 each year. Each player may select among shoe styles previously approved by the League office. All players on the same team must wear shoes with the same dominant color. Approved shoe styles will contain one team color which must be the same for all players on a given team. A player may wear an unapproved standard football shoe style as long as the player tapes over the entire shoe to conform to his team's selected dominant color. Logos, names, or other commercial identification on shoes are not permitted to be visible unless advance approval is granted by the League office (see Article 7). Size and location of logos and names on shoes must be approved by the <u>League office</u>. When a shoe logo or a name approved by the League office is covered with an appropriate use of tape (see Article 4(f)), players will be allowed to cut out the tape covering the original logo or name, provided the cut is clean and is the exact size of the logo or name. The logo or name of the shoe manufacturer must not be reapplied to the exterior of taped shoes unless advance approval is granted by the League office. Kicking shoes must not be modified (including using a shoelace wrapped around toe and/or bottom of the shoe), and any shoe that is worn by a player with an artificial limb on his kicking leg must have a kicking surface that conforms to that of a normal kicking shoe. Punters and placekickers may omit the shoe from the kicking foot in preparation for and during kicking plays. Punters and placekickers may wear any combination of tri-colored shoes provided that the colors are consistent with those selected by the team and with the policy listed above.

Article 4 In addition to the several prohibited items of equipment and apparel specified in Article 3 above, the following are also prohibited:

Projecting Objects

(a) Metal or other hard objects that project from a player's person or uniform, including from his shoes.

Uncovered Hard Objects, Substances

(b) Hard objects and substances, including but not limited to casts, guards or braces for hand, wrist, forearm, elbow, hip, thigh, knee, and shin, unless such items are appropriately covered on all edges and surfaces by a minimum of ⅜-inch foam rubber or similar soft material. Any such item worn to protect an injury must be reported by the applicable coaching staff to the Umpire in advance of the game, and a description of the injury must be provided. If the Umpire determines that an item in question, including tape or bandages on hands or forearms, may present undue risk to other players, he may prevent its use at a time before or during a game until the item is removed or appropriately corrected.

Detachable Toe

(c) Detachable kicking toe.

Torn Items

(d) Torn or improperly fitting equipment creating a risk of injury to other players, e.g. the hard surfaces of shoulder pads exposed by a damaged jersey.

Improper Cleats

(e) Shoe cleats made of aluminum or other material that may chip, fracture, or develop a cutting edge. Conical cleats with concave sides or points which measure less than ⅜-inch in diameter at the tips, or cleats with oblong ends which measure less than ¼- by ¾-inch at the end tips are also prohibited. Nylon cleats with flat steel tips are permitted.

Improper Tape

(f) Opaque, contrasting-color tape that covers any part of the helmet, jersey, pants, stockings, or shoes; transparent tape or tape of the same color as the background material is permissible for use on these items of apparel. Players may use opaque, white, black, or one dominant club color tape on hands and arms, provided it conforms to 5-4-4(b) above ("Uncovered Hard Objects, Substances") and 5-4-4(h) below ("Approved Glove <u>Color</u>"). Opaque tape on shoes is permitted, provided it is the same color as the shoe, and provided it does not carry up into the stocking area.

Items Colored Like Football

(g) Headgear or any other equipment or apparel which, in the opinion of the Referee, may confuse an opponent because of its similarity in color to that of the game football. If such color is worn, it must be broken by stripes or other patterns of sharply contrasting color or colors.

Approved Glove Color

(h) Gloves, wrappings, elbow pads, and other items worn on the arms below or over the jersey sleeves by interior offensive linemen (excluding tight ends) which are of a color different from that which is mandatorily reported to the League office by the club before July 1 each year. Such reported color must be white or other official color of the applicable team, and, once reported, must not be changed throughout that same season. Players at other positions (non-interior linemen) also may wear gloves provided they are a solid white, solid black, or a solid color that is an official color of the applicable club. Gloves may also be a tri-color combination of black, white, and one (1) official color of the applicable club. Gloves may also be a bi-color combination of black or white with one (1) official color of the applicable team. Clubs are not required to designate to the League office by July 1, the color of gloves that will be worn by their non-interior linemen.

Adhesive, Slippery Substances

(i) Adhesive or slippery substances on the body, equipment, or uniform of any player; provided, however, that players may wear gloves with a tackified surface if such tacky substance does not adhere to the football or otherwise cause handling problems for players

Garments Under Jerseys

(j) Quarterbacks will be allowed to wear under the game jersey a solid-color T-shirt, turtleneck, or sweatshirt (consistent with team undergarment color) with sleeves cut to any length, as long as both sleeves are evenly trimmed and the edges are sewn and hemmed. All other players may wear garments under game jerseys only if the undergarment sleeves either (a) do not extend below the sleeves of the jersey; or (b) are full length to the wrist. No other sleeve lengths for garments under jerseys are permitted for players other than quarterbacks. Players may not wear long-sleeved undergarments that include pebble-grip sleeves. Any garments under jerseys that are exposed at the neck or sleeve area and that carry an exposed logo or commercial name must be licensed by and approved by the League Office for wear on the field (see Article 7). All members of the same team who wear approved undergarments with exposed necks or sleeves must wear the same color on a given day, which color must be white or a solid color that is an official team color (solid means that sleeves must not carry stripes, designs, or team names).

Prohibited Headwear Coverings

(k) Players are not permitted to wear bandannas, stockings, or other unapproved headwear anywhere on the field during the pregame, game, or postgame periods, even if such items are worn under their helmet.

Article 5   It is recommended that all players wear hip pads, thigh pads, and knee pads which reasonably avoid the risk of injury. Unless otherwise provided by individual team policy, it is the players' responsibility and decision whether to follow this recommendation and use such pads. If worn, all three forms of pads listed above must be covered by the outer uniform. Basketball-type knee pads are permitted but must also be covered by the outer uniform.

Article 6   Among the types of optional equipment that are permitted to be worn by players are the following:

Rib Protectors

(a) Rib protectors ("flak jackets") under the jersey.

Wristbands

(b) Wristbands, provided they are white or black only.

Towels

(c) Towels, provided they are white licensed towels
approved by the League office for use on the playing
field. Players are prohibited from adding to these
towels personal messages, logos, names, symbols, or
illustrations. Such towels also must be attached to or
tucked into the front waist of the pants, and must be
no larger than 6 x 8 inches (slightly larger size may
be issued to quarterbacks, or may be folded to these
limits for wearing in games). A player may wear no
more than one towel. Players are prohibited from
discarding on the playing field any loose towels or
other materials used for wiping hands and the football. Streamers or ribbons, regardless of length,
hanging from any part of the uniform, including the
helmet, are prohibited.

Headwear

(d) When players are on the field, as defined in Article 1,
during the pregame, game and postgame periods,
they may wear approved caps, approved cold weather
gear, or other approved headwear for medical purposes only, as determined by the Commissioner. Any
permissible <u>headwear</u> must be approved by the
League office, and if worn under the helmet, no
portion may hang from or otherwise be visible
outside the helmet.

Article 7   Throughout the period on game-day that a player is
visible to the stadium and television audience (including
in pregame warm-ups, in the bench area, and during
postgame interviews in the locker room or on the field),
players are prohibited from wearing, displaying, or orally

promoting equipment, apparel, or other items that carry commercial names or logos of companies, unless such commercial identification has been approved in advance by the League office. The size of any approved logo or other commercial identification involved in an agreement between a manufacturer and the League will be modest and unobtrusive, and there is no assurance that it will be visible to the television audience. Subject to any future approved arrangements with a manufacturer and subject to any decision by the Commissioner to suspend enforcement temporarily of this provision governing shoes, visible logos and names of shoes are prohibited, including on the sole of the shoe that may be seen from time to time during the game.

Article 8   Throughout the period on game-day that a player is visible to the stadium and television audience (including in pregame warm-ups, in the bench area, and during postgame interviews in the locker room or on the field), players are prohibited from wearing, displaying, or otherwise conveying personal messages either in writing or illustration, unless such message has been approved in advance by the League office. Items to celebrate anniversaries or memorable events, or to honor or commemorate individuals, such as helmet decals, and arm bands and jersey patches on players' uniforms, are prohibited unless approved in advance by the League office. All such items must relate to team or League events or personages. The League will not grant permission for any club or player to wear, display, or otherwise convey messages, through helmet decals, arm bands, jersey patches, or other items affixed to game uniforms or equipment, which relate to political activities or causes, other non-football events, causes or campaigns, or charitable causes or campaigns. Further, such armbands and jersey patches must be modest in size, tasteful, non-commercial, and non-controversial; must not be worn for more than one football season; and if approved for use by a specific team, must not be worn by players on other teams in the League.

Article 9 Consistent with the equipment and uniform rules of this Section 4, players must otherwise present a professional and appropriate appearance while before the public on game-day. Among the types of activities that are prohibited are use of tobacco products (smokeless included) while in the bench area and use of facial makeup. The Referee is authorized to use his judgment in determining whether any other unusual appearance or behavior is in violation of this Article 9.

Penalties:

(a) For violation of this Section 4 discovered during pregame warmups or at other times prior to the game, player will be advised to make appropriate correction; if violation is not corrected, player will not be permitted to enter the game.

(b) For violation of this Section 4 discovered while player is in game, player will be advised to make appropriate correction at the next change of possession; if violation is not corrected, player will not be permitted to enter the game. Provided, however, if the violation involves the competitive aspects of the game (e.g. illegal kicking toe of shoe, an adhesive or slippery substance), player will be suspended immediately (removed from the game for one play) upon discovery.

(c) For repeat violation: Disqualification from game.

(d) For illegal entry or return of a player suspended under this Section 4: Loss of five yards from

succeeding spot and removal until properly
equipped after one down.

(e) For violation of this Section 4 detected in the bench
area: Player and head coach will be asked to remove
the objectionable item, properly equip the player,
or otherwise correct the violation. The involved
player or players will be disqualified from the game
if correction is not made promptly.

■ Supplemental Notes

*Note 1: In addition to the game-day penalties specified
above, the Commissioner may subsequently impose indepen-
dent disciplinary action on the involved player, up to and
including suspension from the team's next succeeding
game—preseason, regular season, or postseason, whichever is
applicable.*

*Note 2: If a player is suspended (removed from the game for
one play) for having adhesive or slippery substances on his
body, equipment, or uniform, he must remain out of the
game for one play, even if there is a team timeout, the two-
minute warning, or the end of a period.*

*Note 3: If a player (kicker) is suspended (removed from the
game for one play) for having an illegal kicking shoe, he
must remain out of the game for one play, unless there is a
team timeout, the two-minute warning, or the end of the
period.*

Free Kicks

Rule 6

Free Kicks

Section 1 **PROCEDURES FOR A FREE KICK**

Article 1 A free kick is a kickoff or safety kick that puts the ball in play to start a free kick down. It may be made from any point on the kicking (offensive) team's restraining line and between the inbounds lines.

(a) A kickoff puts the ball in play at the start of each half, after a try, and after a successful field goal. A dropkick or placekick may be used for a kickoff.

Note: During a placekick on a kickoff, the kicking team may use a manufactured tee that is one inch in height and approved by the league. Once the ball has been placed on the kicking tee, the kicking tee cannot be moved. If the ball falls off the tee, or the tee is moved, the covering officials must stop play and restart the timing process without penalty to the kicking team. If the ball falls off the tee a second time during the same free kick down, the kicking team then must either use a player to hold the ball or must kick it off the ground. The ball may be placed on the ground leaning against the tee, provided the tee is in its normal upright position.

(b) A safety kick puts the ball in play after a safety. A dropkick, placekick, or punt may be used for a safety kick. A tee cannot be used for a safety kick.

Penalty: For illegal kick on a free kick down: Loss of five yards.

Article 2 The restraining lines for a free kick shall be as follows, unless they are adjusted because of a distance penalty:

(a) The restraining line for the kicking team shall be its 30-yard line for a kickoff and its 20-yard line for a safety kick.

(b) The restraining line for the receiving team shall be the yard line 10 yards in advance of the kicking team's restraining line.

Article 3   When the ball is kicked on a free kick down:

(a) All kicking team (Team A) players must be inbounds and behind the ball when it is kicked, except:
(1) the holder of a placekick (3-24) may be beyond the line, and
(2) the kicker may be beyond the line, provided that his kicking foot is not beyond the line;

(b) At least four players of the kicking team must be on each side of the kicker. At least three players must be lined up outside each inbounds line, one of whom must be outside the yard-line number.

Note: A holder for a free kick counts as one of the required four players, regardless of where he is positioned.

(c) All receiving team (Team B) players must be inbounds and behind their restraining line until the ball is kicked.

Penalty: For a player being beyond the restraining line when the ball is kicked (offside): Loss of five yards.

Penalty: For a player being out of bounds when the ball is kicked: Loss of five yards.

(d) After the ball is kicked, no more than two receiving team players may intentionally form a wedge in an attempt to block for the runner. An illegal wedge is defined as three or more players lined up shoulder-to-shoulder within two yards of each other.

Note: This does not apply when the kicking team lined up in an obvious onside kick formation.

Penalty: For players intentionally forming an illegal wedge: Loss of 15 yards.

Article 4   The following applies to the catch or recovery of a free kick:

(a) If a player of the receiving team catches or recovers the ball, he may advance.

(b) If the ball is declared dead while in the simultaneous possession of two opposing players, the ball is awarded to the receiving team.

(c) A player of the kicking team may legally touch, catch, or recover the ball if:
  (1) it first touches a receiving team player; or
  (2) it reaches or crosses the receiving team's restraining line.

(d) The ball is dead if it is caught or recovered by a player of the kicking team. If the catch or recovery is legal, the ball belongs to the kicking team at the dead-ball spot.

(e) If the ball comes to rest inbounds after reaching the receiving team's restraining line and no player attempts to possess it, the ball becomes dead and belongs to the receiving team at the dead-ball spot.

Note: For illegal catch or recovery, see Section 2, Article 4.

Article 5   It is a touchback if a free kick:

(a) goes out of bounds behind the receiving team's goal line;

(b) strikes the receiving team's goal post, uprights, or crossbar; or

(c) is downed in the end zone by the receiving team.

Article 6   A free kick ends when either team possesses the ball, or when the ball is dead, if that precedes possession. A running play begins when the receiving team establishes possession of the ball.

Section 2   **OTHER FREE KICK FOULS**

Article 1   **Item 1: Kicking Team.** After the ball touches a receiving team player, or has reached the receiver's restraining line, a kicking team player may legally block an opponent, and he may use his hands and arms to push or pull an opponent out of the way in a personal attempt to recover the ball.

Prior to the ball touching a receiving team player or reaching the receiving team's restraining line, he may not block or use his hands or arms against an opponent between the restraining lines, except to push or pull aside a receiver who is actively attempting to obstruct his attempt to proceed downfield.

Regardless of the location of the ball, he may legally block an opponent at or beyond the receiving team's restraining line.

Item 2: Receiving Team. After the ball is kicked, receiving team players can legally block (see Rule 12, Section 1), and they may use their hands/arms legally to push or pull an opponent out of the way in a personal attempt to recover the ball.

Penalty: For illegal blocking or use of hands by either team: Loss of 10 yards. See 12-2-13 for penalty for a low block.

Article 2   A player of the receiving team is not permitted to run into the kicker before he recovers his balance. See also 12-2-8-(h) for personal fouls against the kicker.

Penalty: For running into the kicker: Loss of five yards.

Article 3   The kicking team may not kick the ball out of bounds or be the last to touch the ball before it goes out of bounds between the goal lines. If the receiving team is the last to

---

touch the ball before it goes out of bounds, the receiving team puts the ball in play at the inbounds spot.

Penalty: For a free kick out of bounds: The receiving team may elect to take possession of the ball 30 yards from the spot of the kick or at the out-of-bounds spot.

Article 4   Item 1: A player of the kicking team may not touch, catch, or recover the ball before it has reached the receiving team's restraining line, unless it has first been touched by a receiving team player.

Penalty: For illegal touching of a free kick by the kicking team: Loss of five yards, or the receiving team takes possession of the ball at the spot of the illegal touch.

Item 2: If a kicking team player goes out of bounds during the kick, he may not touch or recover the ball beyond the receiving team's restraining line, unless it has first been touched by a receiving team player. If a kicking team player touches the ball before re-establishing himself legally inbounds, it is a free kick out of bounds.

Penalty: For illegal touching of a free kick by the kicking team: Loss of five yards.

Article 5   If the ball has not been touched by either team after the kick and rolls dead in the field of play before reaching the receiving team's restraining line, it is a foul.

Penalty: For a short free kick: Loss of five yards.

Section 3   **ENFORCEMENT OF FOULS**

Article 1   If there is an accepted foul during a free kick, the normal
              enforcement is from the previous spot, and the free kick
              is made again, unless a foul by the kicking team occurs
              prior to the end of the kick. In such cases, the receiving
              team will have the option of enforcing the penalty at the
              previous spot and replaying the down or adding the
              penalty yardage to the dead-ball spot.

Exceptions:

              (a) A personal foul (blocking) after a fair catch signal is
                  enforced from the spot of the foul.

              (b) A foul for fair catch interference is enforced from the
                  spot of the foul.

              (c) A foul for an invalid fair catch signal is enforced
                  from the spot of the signal.

              (d) For a free kick out of bounds, see Section 2, Article 3.

              (e) For a free kick illegally touched, see Section 2,
                  Article 4.

              (f) Double fouls are enforced according to the normal
                  rules. See Rule 14.

              (g) The dead-ball spot for free kicks that result in a
                  touchback is the 20-yard line.

Scrimmage

Rule 7

Scrimmage

Section 1   **NECESSARY GAIN ON DOWNS**

Article 1   A new series (first-and-10) is awarded to the offensive
team when the following conditions exist; subject,
however, to the specific rules of enforcement
(Rule 14).

(a) When, during a given series, the ball is declared
dead in possession of offensive team while it is on,
above, or across the necessary line, or unless a
penalty places it there, or unless a touchback for
them results.

(b) When the ball is dead in the field of play in the
offense's possession, after having been in the defensive team's possession during the same down.

(c) When a foul is made by the defense, except as otherwise specified (14-8-5), or when an impetus by them
results in a touchback for offensive team.

(d) When the ball is declared dead in possession of the
receiving team after a free kick or scrimmage kick.

(e) When the kicking team recovers a scrimmage kick
anywhere in the field of play after it *first* has been
touched *beyond* the line by the receivers. See 9-3-2-
Item 1.

Article 2   The *forward part of the ball* in its position when declared
dead in the field of play shall be taken as the determining point in measuring any distance gained. *The ball
shall not be rotated when measuring.*

A.R. 7.1   Second-and-10 on B30. Runner A1 goes to
the B25 where he is tackled, fumbles, and defensive

player B1 recovers and runs to B28. B1 fumbles and A2 recovers on the B28 where he is downed.

Ruling: A's ball first-and-10 on B28. The ball is dead in the offensive team's possession after having been in the defensive team's possession during same down.

A.R. 7.2 Second-and-10 on B30. Quarterback A1 throws an incomplete pass. Defensive tackle held the tight end A2 on the line of scrimmage.

Ruling: A's ball first-and-10 on B25. Foul by defense is automatic first down for offensive team unless otherwise specified in 14-8-5.

A.R. 7.3 Fourth-and-10 on A30. A punted ball is muffed by receiver B1 on the B35. A kicking team player A1 recovers on the B30.

Ruling: A's ball first-and-10 on the B30. Kicking team recovers kick first touched by receiver beyond line. The ball is dead when recovered by A1 (9-3-2-Item 1).

A.R. 7.4 Fourth-and-10 on A30. Punt is first touched by kicking team player A1 on B35 and then muffed by receiver B1. Kicker A2 recovers on B30.

Ruling: B's ball first-and-10 on B35. Illegal touch. It was first touched by the kickers and not the receiving team (9-3-2-Item 2).

A.R. 7.5 Fourth-and-10 on A30. A punt is blocked and rolls beyond line to A35 where receiver B1 tries to recover but muffs it back to the A28 where kicker A1 falls on it.

Ruling: A's ball first-and-10 on A28. Ball first touched beyond line by receiver (9-3-2-Item 1).

Article 3 If offensive team fails to advance ball to necessary line during a given series, it is awarded to defensive team for a new series at the spot:

(a) where dead at end of fourth down; or

        (b) where it is placed because of a combination penalty
           (14-8-2) or a touchback for defensive team.

Exceptions: Ball is not awarded to defensive team when
fourth down results either in:

(a) a safety by the offensive team; or

(b) a touchback for the offensive team.

Section 2   **POSITION OF PLAYERS AT SNAP**

Article 1   The offensive team must have:
        (a) seven-or-more players on its line (3-18) at the snap.

        (b) all players who are *not* on line, other than the snap
           receiver under center, must be at least 1-yard behind
           it at snap.

Note: Offensive linemen may lock legs.

A.R. 7.6 Fourth-and-10 on B35. On a field goal attempt
offensive tackle A1 and offensive guard A2 lock their legs
as they line up. The field goal is good.
Ruling: Field goal good, no foul.

Article 2   During a <u>punt,</u> field-goal attempt or a Try Kick, a Team
    B player, who is within one yard of the line of scrim-
    mage at the snap, must have his helmet outside the
    snapper's shoulder pads.

*Note: This restriction does not apply if a team does not
present an apparent punt, field goal, or Try Kick formation,
or if, after the offensive team has assumed a set position,
there is a shift, or a player goes in motion.*

**Penalty: For illegal formation by the defense: Loss of
five yards from previous spot.**

Article 3   After the neutral zone starts, no player of either team at
    snap may:

(a) encroach upon it (3-19); or

(b) be offside (3-20).

Note 1: It is offside when a defender moves beyond the neutral zone prior to the snap and is parallel to or beyond an offensive lineman, with an unabated path to the quarterback or kicker. Even though no contact is made by a blocker; officials are to blow their whistles immediately.

Note 2: It is a Neutral Zone Infraction when a defender enters the neutral zone prior to the snap, causing the offensive player(s) in close proximity to react (move) immediately to protect himself against impending contact; officials are to blow their whistles immediately. If there is no immediate reaction by the offensive player(s) in close proximity, and the defensive player returns to a legal position prior to the snap without contacting an opponent, there is no foul. For offensive linemen aligned from tight end to tight end, a player is in close proximity if he is within 2½ players of another player. A flexed or split receiver is considered to be in close proximity if he is lined up on the side of the ball on which the violation occurs.

Note 3. During the last two minutes of a half, once the ball has been respotted for the succeeding down and the Head Linesman has placed his bean bag on the ground at the new line of scrimmage, the Umpire, upon signal from the Referee, is to step away from the ball. At this point a snap may be made. If the ball is snapped before all members of the defensive team have taken their proper position on line of scrimmage, play is to be stopped immediately and that team penalized five yards for offside.

 Penalty: For encroachment, offside, or a neutral zone infraction: Loss of five yards from previous spot. Number of down and necessary line remain the same.

■ Supplemental Notes

(1) If any player crosses his line and contacts an opponent, it is encroaching. *Blow whistle* immediately on contact.

(2) If a defensive player charges into the neutral zone, and the action draws an immediate reaction by an offensive player in close proximity, the action by the defense is a neutral-zone infraction.

(3) If a player charges into neutral zone without violating items (2) and (3), and returns to a legal position prior to the snap, it is not encroaching unless it is a repeated act after a warning.

A.R. 7.7 Second-and-10 on B30. Defensive tackle B1's initial charge into neutral zone makes offensive guard A1 directly across from him flinch and draw back.
Ruling: Blow the whistle immediately. Penalize B1 for a neutral zone infraction. A's ball second-and-5 on B25.

A.R. 7.8 Second-and-10 on B30. Defensive back B1 runs toward the line of scrimmage as if he is going right over guard A1. He stops on the defensive side of the neutral zone but guard A1 in a three-point stance picks up.
Ruling: Penalize offensive A1 for false start. A's ball second-and-15 on B35. Blow the whistle immediately.

A.R. 7.9 Second-and-10 on A30. Defensive player B1 jumps across the line and contacts offensive player A1 prior to the snap.
Ruling: Blow whistle immediately and kill play. A's ball second-and-five on A35. Encroachment.

A.R. 7.10 Second-and-10 on B35. The offensive team uses a double shift (first, second, or third time during the game). At the start of the second shift, a defensive player B1 charges into the neutral zone and is in the neutral zone at the snap.

Ruling: A's ball second-and-5 from B30. Defense offside.

A.R. 7.11 Second-and-5 on 50. The offensive team uses a double shift. At the start of the second shift, defensive player B1 charges into the neutral zone and makes contact.
Ruling: A's ball first-and-10 on B45. Encroachment.

A.R. 7.12 Third-and-7 on B25. Offensive upback A2 moves abruptly (simulating the snap) when he goes in motion prior to the snap.
Ruling: A's ball third-and-12 on B30. Blow whistle immediately. False start.

Article 4   An offensive player who comes into game wearing an illegal number for the position he takes must report to the Referee who in turn will report same to the defensive captain. The clock shall not be stopped and the ball may not be put in play until the Referee takes his normal position.

Penalties:

a) **Five yards for illegal substitution if player in above category enters the game and/or his team's huddle without reporting and later reports his player position status to the Referee prior to snap.**

b) **For failure to notify Referee of change in eligibility or ineligibility status (when required) prior to snap: Loss of five yards for illegal substitution.**

■ Supplemental Notes

(1) It is not necessary for entering substitutes or players legally in the game to report to the Referee under the following conditions:

---

a) players wearing eligible pass receiver numbers playing in eligible pass receiver positions; or

b) players wearing ineligible pass receiver numbers playing in ineligible pass receiver positions.

(2) When a player is legally designated (Referee informed) as being eligible or ineligible (Article 3), he must participate in such a position until legally withdrawn. If the player remains in this position, he must report on every play.

Exception: If the change in playing position status is followed by: 1) a touchdown; 2) a completed kick from scrimmage (a punt, drop kick, or place kick); 3) a foul; 4) a team time out; 5) the end of a quarter; 6) time out for the two-minute warning; 7) a replay challenge; or 8) change of possession, the said player may return to his originally eligible or ineligible playing position without restriction. However, if the kick is not completed or a touchdown not made, the said player must remain in his new position until legally withdrawn for one down (5-1-5). If withdrawn, he is to re-enter to the position indicated by his number unless he again informs the Referee that he is assuming a position other than that designated by his number.

(3) Coaches must instruct those players wearing numbers not qualifying them for designated positions to report to the Referee, *prior to the huddle*, their change in eligibility or ineligibility status. This rule prevails whether player is already in the game or is an entering substitute and whether it is a play from scrimmage; an attempted field goal; or a Try after touchdown.

(4) The Referee especially must be alert to the above situation at all times and be certain that the defensive

captain is notified of the change of any player position status.

Article 5   At the snap, a center, guard, or tackle of the offensive team may be anywhere on his line, but he may not be behind it unless he is at least 1-yard behind it and has informed the Referee of his change of position to that of an eligible receiver (7-2-3).

Penalty: For center, guard, or tackle not on the line at the snap: Loss of five yards from the previous spot.

A.R. 7.13 Offensive tackle A1 is legally shifted to the backfield and is then withdrawn. He returns before the next snap to a tackle position.
Ruling: Illegal. He must stay out one play, or have his team request a team timeout. See 5-3-2 and 7-2-4-Exc.

Article 6   At the snap, all offensive players must be stationary in their positions:

(a) without any movement of feet, head, or arms;

(b) without swaying of body; and

(c) without moving directly forward *except that one player only and he, playing in a backfield position, may be in motion provided he is moving, parallel to, obliquely backward from, or directly backward from the line of scrimmage at snap.*

Note 1: No player is ever permitted to be moving obliquely or directly forward toward his opponent's goal line at snap.

Note 2: Non-abrupt movement of head and/or shoulders by offensive players prior to the snap is legal. Players must come to a stop before ball is snapped. If officials judge the action of the offensive players to be abrupt, false start foul is to be called.

Penalty: For player illegally in motion at snap: Loss of five yards from previous spot. In case of doubt, this penalty shall be enforced.

A.R. 7.14 Third-and-one on the B40. Quarterback A1 stops about a foot behind the center and then moves forward and takes the snap and goes to the B38.
Ruling: Illegal motion. Can't be moving forward at snap. A's ball third-and-six on B45.

A.R. 7.15 At the snap offensive back A1 is on the line of scrimmage and in motion along line.
Ruling: A1 is illegally in motion as he was not playing a backfield position.

A.R. 7.16 The offensive Team A has eight players on the line. End A1 on line runs behind line to lead interference and at the snap is three yards behind the line.
Ruling: Illegal motion as end A1 was not playing in a backfield position at the snap. The distance behind the line at the snap has no bearing on the validity of this situation.

A.R. 7.17 After a huddle or shift, offensive halfback A1 assumes a position on the end of the line and offensive end A2 assumes a position 1 yard behind the line (no change in their eligibility status). End A2 only in motion parallel to line at snap.
Ruling: End A2 legally in motion as he was playing in a backfield position at the snap.

A.R. 7.18 After a huddle or shift offensive halfback A1 assumes a position on the end of the line and offensive end A2 assumes a position 1 yard behind the line (no change in their eligibility status). Halfback A1 only is in motion parallel to line at snap.
Ruling: A1 illegally in motion as he was not playing in a backfield position at the snap.

Article 7 After a shift or huddle all offensive players after assuming a set position must come to an absolute stop. They also must remain stationary in their position without any movement of their feet, head or arms, or swaying of their body for a period of at least one second before snap.

 Penalty: For illegal pause or motion after a shift: Loss of five yards from previous spot. In case of doubt the penalty is to be enforced.

■ Supplemental Notes

(1) A single man in motion is not a shift, but if he is moving directly forward at the snap, it is illegal motion (7-2-6-c).

(2) After a shift if all players come to a legal stop and then one or more men start again before snap, the play may result in encroaching (7-2-3), illegal motion (7-2-6), a second shift (7-2-7), or a false start (7-3-4).

A.R. 7.19 Team A shifts and comes to a stop for one second. Offensive End A1 then goes out along his line and stops. Back A2 then moves backward and the ball is snapped less than one second after End A1 stops.
Ruling: Legal play. Movement of End A1 and Back A2 are not simultaneous.

A.R. 7.20 After a shift or a huddle the offensive players come to a stop and remain stationary. Before the lapse of 1 second Back A1, who did not shift or huddle, starts and is in motion backward at snap.
Ruling: Illegal shift. All eleven players must come to an absolute stop for one second.

A.R. 7.21 After a legal pause following a shift:

(a) offensive backs A1 and A2 move forward just prior to snap. They regain their positions and are stationary at the snap.

Ruling: A second shift and one second rule again applies.

(b) offensive back A1 charges forward just prior to snap. He regains his position at snap but B1 contacts guard A3 as a result of the movement of A1.

Ruling: Loss of five yards from previous spot against A1 for false start. Blow whistle on contact.

A.R. 7.22 Following a shift or huddle all offensive players except offensive tackle A1 make a legal pause prior to snap. Tackle A1 moves into the neutral zone but regains a stationary position less than one second prior to snap.

Ruling: Illegal shift unless tackle A1 is penalized for false start.

Article 8 No player may be out of bounds at the snap.

Penalty: For player out of bounds at snap: Loss of five yards from the previous spot.

Section 3 **PUTTING THE BALL IN PLAY**

Article 1 The offensive team must put the ball in play with a snap at the spot where the previous down ended, unless the down ended outside the inbounds lines, at which time the ball is put in play by a snap at the nearest inbounds line. If a fair-catch kick is chosen after a fair catch, 10-2-4 and 11-4-3 apply.

Penalty: For not using a snap when prescribed: Loss of five yards.

Article 2 When a foul occurs, the ball shall *not* be put in play again until the penalty (Rule 14):

(a) has been enforced;

(b) declined;

(c) offset;

(d) been annulled by a choice; or

(e) disregarded.

Article 3 The snap (3-32) may be made by any offensive player who is on the line but must conform to the following provisions:

(a) The snap must start with ball on ground with its long axis horizontal and at right angles to line, and

(b) The impulse must be given by one quick and continuous motion of hand or hands of snapper. The ball must actually leave or be taken from his hands during this motion.

(c) The snapper may *not*:
(1) move his feet abruptly from the start of snap until the ball has left his hands;
(2) have quick plays after the neutral zone starts if the officials have not had a reasonable time to assume their normal stances.

Penalty: For illegally snapping ball: Loss of five yards from spot of snap for false start.

Article 4 From the start of the neutral zone until the snap, no offensive player, if he assumed a set position, shall charge or move in such a way as to simulate the start of a play (false start).

Penalty: For false start: Loss of five yards from previous spot.

■ Supplemental Notes

(1) When interior lineman of the offensive team (tackle to tackle) takes or simulates a three-point stance and then moves after taking that stance, the offensive team shall be penalized for a false start. The official *must* blow his whistle immediately.

---

(2) The penalty for a false start (Article 4) shall be enforced regardless of whether snap is made. The distance penalty for the false start may be declined.

(3) Any quick, abrupt movement by a single offensive player or by several offensive players in unison, which simulates the start of the snap is a false start.

Note: Any obvious attempt by the quarterback to draw an opponent offside is a false start penalty.

(4) A player who extends his hands under center as if to receive the snap may go in motion, provided he comes to a complete stop and resets as a back before the ball is snapped. If he fails to reset as a back, it a false start when the ball is snapped. This includes any player under or behind the center who places his hands on his knees or on the body of the center. If the action is quick and abrupt it is a false start.

(5) Any offensive backfield player, not under center, including a kicker or a place kick holder who extends his hands, does not have to receive the snap, nor must he retract them prior to the snap.

A.R. 7.23 Second-and-10 on the B40. Quarterback A1 bobs his head in an exaggerated manner prior to the snap and draws the defense into the neutral zone. **Ruling:** Penalize five yards for false start. Blow the whistle immediately.

A.R. 7.24 Second-and-10 on A30. Offensive interior lineman A1 simulates a three-point stance after a huddle. He then moves to a regular three-point stance. Defensive player charges and contacts player not directly opposite him. **Ruling:** False start against offense. Blow whistle immediately to kill play. Defensive action ignored. A's ball second-and-15 on A25.

A.R. 7.25 Second and 10 on A30. Offensive team breaks from huddle and all linemen except tackle A1 assume a three-point stance. Tackle A1 rests his elbows on his knees in a crouched position. After a second A1 assumes a three-point stance. When he started his move to a three-point stance defensive B1 charges across line and contacts tackle A1.

Ruling: Penalize B1 for encroachment. A1's move was legal. Blow the whistle immediately. A's ball second-and-five on A35.

A.R. 7.26 Second-and-10 on A30. Offensive interior lineman moves his feet abruptly after taking a three-point stance to make himself more comfortable. The ball is then snapped and defensive player B1 gets quarterback A2 to fumble and B1 recovers on A25.

Ruling: False start. Blow whistle immediately on lineman's movement.

A.R. 7.27 Third-and-10 on A30. Offensive quarterback A1 places his hands on side of snapper. Ball goes through A1's legs to Back A2 who completes a pass to the A40.

Ruling: Backward pass. A's ball first-and-10 on A40.

A.R. 7.28 The offensive team comes out of a huddle into a T formation. Quarterback A1 extends his hands under the center, after which the offensive team shifts into a spread formation, with quarterback A1 assuming a blocking halfback position. Offensive back A2 assumes a tailback position with hands extended for the snap. During the shift into the spread formation by the offensive team, defensive B1 is drawn offside.

Ruling: False start against the offensive team. Blow whistle immediately. Loss of five yards. If the defensive team were not offside, it would be a legal play.

Article 5 Prior to the snap no defensive player shall enter the neutral zone and touch the ball.

Penalty: For actions interfering with the ball prior to or during the snap: Loss of five yards for delay from the previous spot. Blow whistle immediately on contact.

Article 6 The snap must be to a player who was *not* on his line at the snap, unless it has first struck the ground. The play continues as after any other backward pass (8-7-1) if the snap either:

(a) first touches the ground; or

(b) first touched or is caught by an eligible backfield receiver.

Penalty: For snapping to ineligible snap receiver: Blow whistle. Loss of five yards from the previous spot.

A.R. 7.29 Fourth-and-10 on A30. The snap first touches the ground and goes off kicker A1's hands. A defensive player picks it up on the A20 and scores.
Ruling: Touchdown (8-7-1)

A.R. 7.30 Fourth-and-10 on A30. Snap is high and punter A1 jumps high and muffs the ball, which rolls to the A20. A defensive player B1 picks up the ball on the A20 and scores.
Ruling: Touchdown. (8-7-1)

Article 7 Ball is next put in play (snap) at inbounds spot by the team entitled to possession (7-1-1 and 7-1-3; and 7-3-1) when:

(a) a loose ball is out of bounds between goal lines;

(b) a runner is out of bounds between goal lines;

(c) the ball is dead in a side zone;

(d) the ball is placed there as the result of an enforcement; or

(e) the mark of a fair catch is in a side zone.

Exceptions: The ball is next put in play at the previous spot if:

(a) a forward pass goes out of bounds;

(b) a forward pass falls incomplete; or

(c) a foul by the defense occurs in a side zone during an unsuccessful Try.

Section 4   **DEAD BALL**

Article 1   An official shall declare dead ball and the down ended:

(a) when a runner is out of bounds or declares himself down by falling to the ground and makes no effort to advance.

(b) any time a quarterback immediately drops to his knee (or simulates dropping his knee) to the ground behind the line of scrimmage during the last two minutes of a half. The game clock will not stop during this action.

(c) whenever a runner declares himself down by sliding feet first on the ground. The ball is dead at the spot of the ball at the instant the runner so touches the ground.

Note: Since the down is over when any part of a sliding runner's body, other than his hands or feet touches the ground, defenders are required to treat a sliding runner as they would a downed runner

(1) A defender must pull up when a runner begins a feet-first slide. That does not mean that all contact by a defender is illegal. If a defender has already committed

> *himself, and the contact is unavoidable, it is not a foul unless the defender makes some other act, such as helmet-to-helmet contact or by driving his forearm into the head or neck area of the runner.*
>
> *(2) A runner who desires to take advantage of the protection provided to a sliding runner is responsible for starting his slide before contact by a defensive player is imminent; if he does not, and waits until the last moment to begin his slide, he puts himself in jeopardy of being tackled like a regular ball carrier.*

(d) when a runner is so held or otherwise restrained that his forward progress ends.

(e) when a runner is contacted by a defensive player and he touches the ground with any part of his body except his hands or feet, ball shall be declared dead immediately.

Note: The ball is dead at the spot of the ball at the instant the runner so touches the ground, irrespective of the condition of the field. A runner touching the ground with his hands or feet while in the grasp of an opponent may continue to advance.

(f) when an opponent takes a ball (hand in hand) in possession of a runner who is down on the ground.

Note: An opponent may take or grab a ball (hand to hand) in possession of a runner provided the runner is on his feet or is airborne.

(g) when any forward pass (legal or illegal) is incomplete (8-1-4).

(h) when any legal kick touches receivers' goal posts or crossbar unless it later scores a goal from field (9-4-2).

(i) when any scrimmage kick that has not been touched by a player of the receiving team crosses the receiver's

goal line from the impetus of the kick and no
attempt is made to run it out, or when it touches the
ground or a player of the kicking team.

(j) when any legal kick or a short free kick is recovered
by the kickers, except one kicked from behind line
which is recovered behind line (not a Try-kick). See
9-3-2-Item 3 for exception.

(k) when defense gains possession during a Try, or a
Try-kick ceases to be in play.

(l) when a touchdown, touchback, safety, field goal, or
Try has been made.

(m) when any receiver catches or recovers the ball after a
fair catch signal (valid or invalid) before kick is
touched by an opponent.

(n) when any official sounds his whistle, even though
inadvertently.

(o) when any fourth down fumble by offensive team is
recovered or caught by any offensive player other
than the fumbling player (8-7-5).

(p) when the ball is out of bounds.

(q) when a runner's helmet comes completely off.

*Note: The game clock will not stop when this occurs, and
the play clock will be reset to 40 seconds. Penalty enforcement following play is as ordinary for fouls during runs or
kicks.*

A.R. 7.31 A runner (in full possession of the ball) is contacted by an opponent while he is attempting to gain
yardage. The contact causes the runner to hit the
ground, at which time the ball comes loose.
Ruling: Play is dead when the impact jars the ball loose.
No fumble.

A.R. 7.32 Second-and-10 on A30. Offensive End A1 catches a legal forward pass on the A40 where he is stopped by B1, but A1 breaks away and goes back to the A38 in an attempt to break loose. He is tackled on the A38 by B2.

Ruling: A's ball third-and-two on A38. No forward progress is given as he was not stopped. He broke away before he was downed.

A.R. 7.33 Second-and-10 on A30. Both eligible offensive A1 and defensive B1 leap in the air to catch a forward pass and collide during a legal attempt to catch ball on the 50. A1 controls the pass and falls to the ground.

Ruling: Ball is dead at spot. A's ball first-and-10 on the 50.

A.R. 7.34 Second-and-10 on A30. Runner A1 breaks clear and is on the 50 when he slips and falls down. B1 takes the ball from A1's hands when A1 is on the ground.

Ruling: Blow whistle to kill play. May not take ball unless runner is on his feet. A's ball first-and-10 on the 50.

A.R. 7.35 Second-and-10 on A30. A backward pass from the A25 hits the ground on the A20 where a defensive player recovers and runs for a score.

Ruling: Touchdown (8-7-1).

A.R. 7.36 Second-and-goal on B4. Runner A1 gets to the goal line and ball touches goal line when he is tackled. He fumbles and defensive B1 recovers in end zone.

Ruling: Touchdown. Ball dead as soon as ball touches goal line in player possession (11-2-1-a).

Article 2   If a loose ball comes to rest anywhere in field and no player attempts to recover, official covering the play should pause momentarily before signaling dead ball (official's timeout). Any legal kick is awarded to receivers and any other ball to team last in possession. When awarded to a team behind the goal line, the ball is placed on its 1-yard line. See 7-4-5 and Note.

A.R. 7.37 Second-and-goal on B2. Runner A1 goes to the line of scrimmage where he is tackled and fumbles. The ball rolls into the end zone when the Referee inadvertently blows his whistle as the ball is loose in the end zone. Defense then falls on the ball.
Ruling: A's ball second-and-goal on B2 (inadvertent whistle).

A.R. 7.38 A player recovers a loose ball in play by falling on it. He then arises and advances.
Ruling: Legal advance unless he has recovered a legal kick made by his team.

Article 3   If a loose ball in play strikes a video board, guide wire, sky cam, or any other object, the ball will be dead immediately, and the down will be replayed at the previous spot.

> *Note 1: If there is not an on-field ruling that the ball struck an object, the Replay Assistant is empowered to initiate a booth review, even if the event occurs prior to the two-minute warning. If, prior to the two-minute warning, no booth review is initiated by the Replay Assistant, a coach's challenge is permitted under the established rules for such a challenge.*

> *Note 2: In the event the down is replayed, the game clock will be reset to the time remaining when the snap occurred. All penalties will be disregarded, except for personal fouls which will be administered prior to the replaying of the down.*

Article 4   If an official inadvertently sounds his whistle during a play, the ball becomes dead immediately:

(a) If the ball is in player possession, the team in possession may elect to put the ball in play where it has been declared dead or to replay the down.

(b) If the ball is a loose ball resulting from a fumble, backward pass, or illegal pass, the team last in possession may elect to put the ball in play at the spot possession was lost or to replay the down.

(c) If the ball is a loose ball resulting from a legal forward pass, a free kick, or a scrimmage kick, the ball is returned to the previous spot, and the down is replayed.

(d) If there is a foul by either team during any of the above, penalty enforcement is as usual during a run, forward pass, kick, fumble, and backward pass.

Note: Penalty enforcement following play blown dead by an inadvertent whistle is as ordinary for fouls during runs, passes, kicks, fumbles, and backward passes.

A.R. 7.39 Second-and-10 on A30. Runner A2 fumbles a handoff from Quarterback A1 on the A25. The ball is on the A22 when the Referee inadvertently blows his whistle.
Ruling: A's ball second-and-10 on A30 (replay).

A.R. 7.40 Second-and-five on A30. During a forward pass, while the ball is in the air, the line judge inadvertently blows his whistle. Prior to the whistle Guard A1 held B1 on the A25.
Ruling: A's ball second-and-15 on A20.

A.R. 7.41 A forward pass is intentionally touched by ineligible A1 beyond line. While the pass is still in flight, a whistle sounds. The pass is incomplete.
Ruling: Replay down. Touch occurred after whistle.

Article 5   When the ball is dead, it is next put in play (7-3-1) at spot designated by official so declaring it. This is usually the spot of the ball when his whistle sounded, but may be some other spot, in case Referee is informed by an official that the ball should have been dead at another spot or in case the rules prescribe otherwise (15-2-3).

Article 6   The ball is not dead because of touching an official who is inbounds or because of a signal by an official other than a whistle.

Note: When a foul occurs, any official observing it immediately sounds his whistle if it is one for which ball remains dead or is dead immediately. Otherwise he signals it by means of dropping his flag (15-1-4-Note) at the spot of the foul unless distance precludes it. In such case, he still indicates the foul in the same manner, but approximates spot, and notes any pertinent circumstances. Unless a whistle sounds, ball continues in play until otherwise dead (7-4-1).

Section 5   POSSESSION OF BALL AFTER OUT OF BOUNDS

Article 1   If any kick, except for a free kick, is out of bounds between the goal lines, ball is next put in play at inbounds spot by the receivers, *unless* there is a spot of illegal touching nearer kickers' goal line. For free kick out of bounds, see 6-2-3.

Article 2   If it is a play from scrimmage, any possession by offensive team after an out of bounds during fourth down is governed by the location of the necessary line (7-1-3).

Article 3   If a runner (3-28) is out of bounds between goal lines, the ball is next put in play by his team at inbounds spot.

Article 4   If a forward pass is out of bounds between the goal lines, the ball is next put in play by passing team as provided for an incompletion or for an illegal pass. See 8-1-4.

Article 5   If a backward pass is out of bounds between the goal lines, the ball is next in play at the inbounds spot by the team last in possession.

Article 6   A fumble by the offensive team cannot result in an advance by that team if the ball is not recovered in the field of play or end zone.

(a) A fumble that goes forward and out of bounds is to return to that team at the spot of the fumble.

(b) A fumble in the field of play that goes backward and out of bounds belongs to the offense at the out-of-bounds spot.

(c) A fumble in the field of play that goes forward into the opponent's end zone and over the end line or sideline results in the ball being given over to the defensive team and a touchback awarded.

(d) A fumble which occurs in a team's own end zone and goes forward into the field of play and out of bounds will result in a safety *if that team provided the impetus that put the ball into the end zone. If the impetus was provided by the opponent, the play will result in a touchback.*

(e) A fumble which occurs in a team's own end zone or in the field of play and the ball goes out of bounds in the end zone will result in a safety *if that team provided the impetus that put the ball into the end zone. If the impetus was provided by the opponent, the play will result in a touchback.*

A.R. 7.42 Second-and-goal on B4. Runner A1 fumbles at line of scrimmage where ball rolls out of bounds:

a) at 1-yard line.
    Ruling: A's ball third-and-goal on B4.

b) over end line.
    Ruling: B's ball first-and-10 on B20.

A.R. 7.43 Second-and-14 on A2. Runner A1 fumbles in end zone. Ball rolls out of bounds.

a) at 1-yard line.
    Ruling: Safety

b) in end zone.
    Ruling: Safety

A.R. 7.44 Second-and-14 on A2. B1 intercepts a forward pass on the A20, runs to the A3, and fumbles. The ball rolls into the end zone. A1 picks up the ball in the end zone, is tackled there, and fumbles ball in end zone. The ball rolls out of bounds over the end line. **Ruling:** Touchback. A's ball-first-and-10 on A20. (See 7-5-6-e).

A.R. 7.45 Third-and-12 on B22. B1 intercepts forward pass in end zone. Tries to run it out and fumbles in end zone. Ball rolls out of bounds:

a) on B3.
    Ruling: Touchback (see 7-5-6-d).

b) over the end line.
    Ruling: Touchback (see 7-5-6-d).

Article 7 If a pass, kick, or fumble is out of bounds behind a goal line, Rule 11 governs.

Forward Pass, Backward Pass, Fumble

Rule 8

Forward Pass, Backward Pass, Fumble

Section 1   **FORWARD PASS**

Article 1   **Definition.** It is a forward pass if:

(a) the ball initially moves forward (to a point nearer the opponent's goal line) after leaving the passer's hand(s); or

(b) the ball first strikes the ground, a player, an official, or anything else at a point that is nearer the opponent's goal line than the point at which the ball leaves the passer's hand(s).

Note: A ball that is intentionally fumbled and goes forward is a forward pass. A ball that is intentionally muffed, and goes forward or backward, is a batted ball (12-1-8). The direction taken by a fumbled or muffed ball does not affect the application of the rules specific to such acts, unless it is ruled that they are intentional.

When a player is in control of the ball and attempting to pass it forward, any intentional forward movement of his hand starts a forward pass.

(a) If the passer is attempting to throw a forward pass, but contact by an opponent materially affects him, causing the ball to go backward, it is a forward pass, regardless of where the ball strikes the ground, a player, an official, or anything else.

(b) If, after an intentional forward movement of his hand, the passer loses possession of the ball as he is attempting to tuck it back toward his body, it is a forward pass. If the player loses possession after he has tucked the ball into his body, it is a fumble.

(c) If the passer loses possession of the ball while attempting to recock his arm, it is a fumble.

Article 2   **Legal Forward Pass.** The offensive team may make one forward pass from behind the line during each <u>down</u>. If the ball, whether in player possession or loose, crosses the line of scrimmage, a forward pass is not permissible, regardless of whether the ball returns behind the line of scrimmage before the pass is thrown.

Item 1: Illegal Passes. Any other forward pass by either team is illegal and is a foul by the passing team, including the following:

(a) A forward pass thrown when the passer is beyond the line of scrimmage.

Note: It is a forward pass from beyond the line of scrimmage if the passer's entire body and the ball are beyond the line of scrimmage when the ball is released, whether the passer is airborne or touching the ground. The penalty for a forward pass thrown from beyond the line is enforced from the spot where the ball is released.

(b) A second forward pass thrown from behind the line of scrimmage.

(c) A forward pass thrown after the ball has crossed the line of scrimmage and has returned behind it.

(d) A forward pass thrown after there has been a change of possession.

Item 2: Intercepted Illegal Pass. If an illegal pass is caught or intercepted, the ball may be advanced and the penalty declined.

Penalties:

(a) **For a forward pass from beyond the line: Loss of down and five yards from the spot of the pass. See 14-8-2. See S.N. 3 below.**

(b) For a second forward pass from behind the line, or for a forward pass that was thrown after the ball returned behind the line: Loss of five yards.

(c) For a forward pass that is thrown by Team B, or for a forward pass that is thrown by Team A after a change of possession: Loss of five yards from the spot of the pass.

■ Supplemental Notes

(1) Eligibility, pass interference, and intentional grounding rules apply when a forward pass is thrown from behind the line, regardless of whether the pass is an illegal forward pass. Eligibility, pass interference, and intentional grounding rules do not apply if a forward pass is thrown (a) from beyond the line, (b) on a Free Kick play, (c) on a Fair Catch kick play, or (d) after a change of possession.

(2) Roughing the passer rules apply on all passes (legal or illegal) thrown from behind the line of scrimmage (<u>12-2-13</u>). If a pass is thrown from beyond the line of scrimmage, unnecessary roughness may apply for action against the passer.

(3) When a distance penalty in Penalty (a) leaves the ball in advance of the necessary line to gain, it is first-and-10 for the offensive team.

(4) See 3-2-3 for the definition of team possession during a forward pass (a loose ball), or for when possession ends.

A.R. 8.1 Second-and-10 on A40. A forward pass is batted back by a defensive player. The ball goes back in the air to the quarterback behind his line. He throws it again to his end who catches it on the B40 and goes for a score.
Ruling: No score. Second-and-15 on A35.

A.R. 8.2 Second-and-18 on A4. A second forward pass from behind <u>A's goal</u> line is caught by offensive end A1 <u>at the A8, where he is tackled</u>.
Ruling: Safety. Safety kick A20 or second-and-20 on A2.

A.R. 8.3 Second-and-10 on A40. A second forward pass from behind the line is intercepted by the defensive team at midfield. A defensive player returns it for a touchdown.
Ruling: Touchdown. Illegal passes may be caught or intercepted.

A.R. 8.4 A punt is caught on the receiving team's 20-yard line. The player who caught the ball attempts to throw a backward pass, but the ball goes forward and hits the ground. The kicking team falls on it.
Ruling: Illegal forward pass. The ball is dead when it hits the ground. Penalize from the spot of the pass. B's ball first-and-10 on B15 (<u>8-1-2-Pen. c</u>).

A.R. 8.5 A forward pass is intercepted by a defensive player in his end zone. While in the end zone, he attempts to pass backward. The pass goes forward, hits the ground on the 1yard line and is recovered by the first passing team.
Ruling: Safety. Forward pass not from scrimmage in the end zone.

A.R. 8.6 Third-and-10 on B35. A second forward pass is thrown from behind the line to flanker A1. Defensive player B1 interferes with A1 on the B20, but A1 catches it anyway and is downed on the B20.
Ruling: Double foul. Illegal pass by the offensive team and interference by the defensive team. Interference rules apply on the second forward pass from behind the line (14-3-1). A's ball third-and-10 on B35 (replay).

A.R. 8.7 Third-and-15 on A30. During a forward pass from beyond the line on the A40, offensive player A1 clips on the A40. The pass is incomplete.
Ruling: Choice for defensive team. Loss of down and five from the spot of the pass or loss of 15 from the spot of the pass (unless offensive player fouls behind that spot— spot of foul). A's ball fourth-and-10 on A35 or third-and-20 on A25.

A.R. 8.8 Third-and-15 on A30. During a forward pass from beyond the line on the A40, defensive player B1 <u>tackles A8 by the facemasks</u> on the A40. The ball falls incomplete.
Ruling: Double foul (14-3-1). Replay at the previous spot. A's ball third-and-15 on A30.

Article 3 **Completed or Intercepted Pass.** A player who makes a catch may advance the ball. A forward pass is complete (by the offense) or intercepted (by the defense) if a player, who is inbounds:

(a) secures control of the ball in his hands or arms prior to the ball touching the ground; and

(b) touches the ground inbounds with both feet or with any part of his body other than his hands.

Note: If a player has control of the ball, a slight movement of the ball will not be considered a loss of possession. He must lose control of the ball in order to rule that there has been a loss of possession.

If the player loses the ball while simultaneously touching both feet or any part of his body other than his hands to the ground, or if there is any doubt that the acts were simultaneous, it is not a catch.

Item 1: Player Going to the Ground. If a player goes to the ground in the act of catching a pass (with or without contact by an opponent), he must maintain control of the ball after he touches the ground, whether in the field of play or the end zone. If he loses control of the ball, and the ball touches the ground before he regains control, the pass is incomplete. If he regains control prior to the ball touching the ground, the pass is complete.

Item 2: Sideline Catches. If a player goes to the ground out-of-bounds (with or without contact by an opponent) in the process of making a catch at the sideline, he must retain control of the ball throughout the act of falling to the ground and after hitting the ground, or the pass is incomplete.

Item 3: End Zone Catches. If a player catches the ball while in the end zone, both feet must be completely on the ground before losing possession, or the pass is incomplete.

Note: In the field of play, if a catch of a forward pass has been completed, after which contact by a defender causes the ball to become loose before the runner is down by contact, it is a fumble, and the ball remains alive. In the end zone, the same action is a touchdown, since the receiver completed the catch beyond the goal line prior to the loss of possession, and the ball is dead when the catch is completed.

Item 4: Ball Touches Ground. If the ball touches the ground after the player secures control of it, it is a catch, provided that the player continues to maintain control.

Item 5: Simultaneous Catch. If a pass is caught simultaneously by two eligible opponents, and both players retain it, the ball belongs to the passers. It is not a simultaneous catch if a player gains control first and an opponent subsequently gains joint control. If the ball is muffed after simultaneous touching by two such players, all the players of the passing team become eligible to catch the loose ball.

Item 6: Carried Out of Bounds. If a player, who is in possession of the ball, is held up and carried out of bounds by an opponent before both feet or any part of his body other than his hands touches the ground inbounds, it is a completed or intercepted pass.

Article 4 **Incomplete Pass.** Any forward pass (legal or illegal) is incomplete and the ball is dead immediately if the pass strikes the ground or goes out of bounds. <u>An incomplete pass is a loss of down, and the ball returns to the previous spot.</u>

Note: If there is any question whether a forward pass is complete, intercepted, or incomplete, it is to be ruled incomplete.

Article 5 **Eligible Receivers.** The following players are eligible to catch a forward pass that is thrown from behind the line of scrimmage.

(a) Defensive players.

(b) Offensive players who are on either end of the line, provided they either have the numbers of eligible players (1-49 and 80-89) or have legally reported to play a position on the end of the line. See 5-1-2 and 7-2-4.

(c) Offensive players who are legally at least one yard behind the line at the snap, provided they either have the numbers of eligible players (1-49 and 80-89) or have legally reported to play a position in the backfield. See 7-2-4.

(d) All other offensive players after the ball has been touched by any defensive player or any eligible offensive player.

Article 6 **Ineligible Receivers.** All offensive players other than those identified in Article 5 above are ineligible to catch a legal or illegal forward pass thrown from behind the line of scrimmage, including:

(a) Players who are not on either end of their line or at least one yard behind it when the ball is snapped.

(b) Offensive players wearing numbers 50-79, unless they have reported a change in their eligibility status to the Referee and have assumed a position on their line or in their backfield as required by Article 5;

(c) Players who fail to notify the Referee of being eligible when required (7-2-4).

(d) An eligible receiver who has been out of bounds prior to or during a pass, even if he has re-established himself inbounds with both feet or with any part of his body other than his hands.

Exception: If an eligible receiver is forced out of bounds by a foul by a defender, including illegal contact, defensive holding, or defensive pass interference, he will become eligible to legally touch the pass (without prior touching by another eligible receiver or defender) as soon as he re-establishes himself inbounds with both feet or with any part of his body other than his hands. See Article 8, Note 3.

(e) A player who takes his stance behind center as a T-formation quarterback is not an eligible receiver unless, before the ball is snapped, he legally moves to a position at least one yard behind the line of scrimmage or on the end of the line, and is stationary in that position for at least one second before the snap.

Note: If he leaves his position behind the center and does not receive the snap, it is a false start unless he has been stationary for at least one second.

Article 7   **Legal Touching.** A forward pass (legal or illegal) thrown
from behind the line may be touched by any eligible
player. A pass in flight may be tipped, batted, or deflected
in any direction by any eligible player at any time,
including such a pass in the end zone. See <u>12-1-8</u>.

Article 8   **Illegal Touching of a Forward Pass.** It is a foul for
illegal touching if a forward pass (legal or illegal), thrown
from behind the line of scrimmage:

(a) is first touched intentionally or is caught by an ineligible offensive player; or

(b) first touches or is caught by an eligible receiver who
has gone out of bounds, either of his own volition or
by being legally forced out of bounds, and has re-
established himself inbounds.

Penalty: Loss of five yards.

*Note 1: If a forward pass (legal or illegal) is caught by an
ineligible offensive player, the ball remains alive.*

*Note 2: The bat of a pass in flight by any player does not
end a pass, nor does it change the impetus if the bat sends it
in touch.*

*Note 3: If a player touches the ball after having been out of
bounds, but prior to re-establishing himself inbounds with
both feet or any part of his body other than his hands, the pass
is incomplete, and there is no penalty for illegal touching.*

A.R. 8.9 Third-and-10 on B40. A forward pass from
behind the line goes off eligible offensive end A1's hands
and flanker back A2 catches it in the end zone.
Ruling: Touchdown.

A.R. 8.10 While in midair, a receiver firmly takes hold
of a pass, but loses possession of the ball when his shoulder lands on the ground with or without being contacted
by an opponent.

Ruling: Incomplete pass. Receiver must hold onto the ball when he alights on the ground in order to complete the reception.

A.R. 8.11 Third-and-10 on B40. On a legal forward pass, eligible end A1 is blocked out of bounds on the B36. He returns to the field of play, catches pass, and scores.
Ruling: No score. The player became an ineligible receiver by going out of bounds. A's ball third-and-15 on B45.

A.R. 8.12 Third-and-10 on B40. On a legal forward pass, eligible end A1 steps out of bounds on the B20. He returns to the field of play and catches a pass after a defensive player touched it. He scores.
Ruling: Touchdown. Legal play as all ineligible receivers become eligible after the defense touches the ball.

A.R. 8.13 Third-and-10 on B40. Eligible end A1 touches a legal forward pass on the B35 and the ball is then touched by ineligible receiver A2 on B35. A defensive player intercepts. He runs it back to the B45 where he fumbles and passing Team A recovers.
Ruling: Legal touch. A's ball first-and-10 on B45

A.R. 8.14 Second-and-five on B20. A forward pass from behind the line barely touches the crossbar. Eligible offensive end A1 catches the ball in the end zone.
Ruling: No score. The ball is dead immediately upon touching the crossbar (or goal posts). Loss of down from the previous spot. A's ball third-and-five on B20.

A.R. 8.15 Second-and-10 on B30. A legal forward pass is caught by offensive flanker A1 near the sideline. His second step touches the sideline.
Ruling: Incomplete pass. Both feet have to land inbounds. A's ball third-and-10 on B30.

A.R. 8.16 Second-and-10 on B30. A legal forward pass is intercepted by defensive player B1. As he lands with the ball in his possession, he straddles the sideline.
Ruling: Incomplete pass. Both feet have to touch inbounds. A's ball third-and-10 on B30.

A.R. 8.17 Second-and-10 on B30. A legal forward pass is intercepted by defensive player B1 who jumped in from out of bounds to intercept pass. Both feet touch inbounds after interception.
Ruling: Incomplete pass. Both feet have to be inbounds prior to interception. A's ball third-and-10 on B30. See 8-1-8 Note 3.

A.R. 8.18 Second-and-10 on B30. Eligible offensive A1 jumps in air (behind or beyond line) to receive a forward pass and then passes backward to ineligible offensive A2 before he lands.
Ruling: Legal catch.

A.R. 8.19 Second-and-20 on A40. Quarterback A1 receives a hand-to-hand snap from center and hands off to back A2 who runs to his right and throws a legal forward pass from behind the line to Quarterback A1. Quarterback A1 catches the pass on the A38 and runs to the 50.
Ruling: A's ball second-and-25 on A35 or A's ball third-and-10 on 50.

A.R. 8.20 Second-and-10 on A40. A legal forward pass touches ineligible guard A1 behind the line. The ball is then intercepted by a defensive player who returns it to the A20.
Ruling: Pass not incomplete when A1 touched by ball. Pass continues in play. B's ball first-and-10 on A20.

A.R. 8.21 Second-and-10 on A40. A legal forward pass is intentionally touched by ineligible guard A1 behind the line. The ball is then intercepted by the defensive

team which returns it to the <u>A30</u>, fumbles, and the ball is recovered by the passing team at the <u>A28</u>.
Ruling: Five-yard penalty for touching ineligible receiver behind the line. A's ball second-and-15 on A35.

A.R. <u>8.22</u> Second-and-10 on A40. A legal forward pass is intentionally touched by ineligible guard A1 behind the line and is then caught by eligible back A2 who runs to the 50.
Ruling: A's ball second-and-15 on A35.

A.R. <u>8.23</u> Fourth-and-two on B4. A legal forward pass touches ineligible receiver A1 in the end zone and falls incomplete.
Ruling: B's ball first-and-10 on B4 (declined).

A.R. <u>8.24</u> Fourth-and-two on B4. A legal forward pass accidentally touches ineligible receiver A1 on the B3 and falls incomplete.
Ruling: B's ball first-and-10 on B4 (declined).

A.R. <u>8.25</u> Second-and-15 on A8. A legal forward pass is batted back by a defensive player and the ball lands in the end zone. A defensive player falls on it in the end zone.
Ruling: Incomplete pass, A's ball third-and-15 on A8.

A.R. <u>8.26</u> First-and-10 on A30. A legal forward pass is touched simultaneously by two opposing eligible players, A1 and B1. The pass goes in the air where ineligible A2 catches it on the A40 and runs to midfield.
Ruling: A's ball first-and-10 on 50.

Section 2   **INTENTIONAL GROUNDING**

Article 1   **Definition.** It is a foul for intentional grounding if a passer, facing an imminent loss of yardage because of pressure from the defense, throws a forward pass without a realistic chance of completion. A realistic chance of completion is defined as a pass that lands in the direction and the vicinity of an originally eligible receiver.

Item 1: Passer or Ball Outside Tackle Position. Intentional grounding will not be called when a passer, who is outside, or has been outside, the tackle position throws a forward pass that lands at or beyond the line of scrimmage, even if no offensive player(s) have a realistic chance to catch the ball (including when the ball lands out of bounds over the sideline or endline). If a loose ball leaves the area bordered by the tackles, this area no longer exists; if the ball is recovered, all intentional grounding rules apply as if the passer is outside this area.

Item 2: Physical Contact. Intentional grounding should not be called if the passer initiates his passing motion toward an eligible receiver and then is significantly affected by physical contact from a defensive player that causes the pass to land in an area that is not in the direction and vicinity of an eligible receiver.

Item 3: Stopping Clock. A player under center is permitted to stop the game clock legally to save time if, immediately upon receiving the snap, he begins a continuous throwing motion and throws the ball directly into the ground.

Item 4: Delayed Spike. A passer, after delaying his passing action for strategic purposes, is prohibited from throwing the ball to the ground in front of him, even though he is under no pressure from defensive rusher(s).

Penalty:

For intentional grounding:

(a) loss of down and 10 yards from the previous spot; or

(b) loss of down at the spot of the foul; or

(c) if the passer is in his end zone when the ball is thrown, it is a safety.

A.R. 8.27 Second-and-20 on A4. A quarterback drops back into his end zone. Just before he is tackled in his end zone, he intentionally grounds the ball by throwing a pass directly in front of him. A defensive player falls on it.
Ruling: Intentional grounding. Safety.

A.R. 8.28 Second-and-10 on A30. Quarterback intentionally grounds ball forward as he stands on A16 to keep from being tackled.
Ruling: Loss of down at spot of foul as quarterback is more than 10 yards behind the line. Third-and-24 on A16.

A.R. 8.29 Second-and-10 on B20. Quarterback deliberately throws the ball out of bounds to stop the game clock.
Ruling: The pass was not thrown away to prevent loss of yardage. A's ball third-and-10 on B20. See 8-3-1-Note 1.

Section 3   **INELIGIBLE PLAYER DOWNFIELD**

Article 1   **Legal and Illegal Acts.** On a scrimmage play during which a legal forward pass is thrown, an ineligible offensive player, including a T-formation quarterback, is not permitted to move more than one yard beyond the line of scrimmage before the pass has been thrown.

Item 1: Legally Downfield. An ineligible player is not illegally downfield if, after initiating contact with an opponent within one yard of the line of scrimmage during his initial charge:

(a) he moves more than one yard beyond the line while legally blocking or being blocked by an opponent; or

(b) after breaking legal contact with an opponent more than one yard beyond the line of scrimmage, he remains stationary until a forward pass is thrown; or

(c) after losing legal contact with an opponent more than one yard beyond the line of scrimmage, he is forced behind the line of scrimmage by an opponent, at which time he is again subject to normal blocking restrictions for an ineligible offensive player.

Note: If an offensive player moves beyond the line while legally blocking or being blocked by an opponent, an eligible offensive player may catch a pass between them and the line of scrimmage.

Item 2: Illegally Downfield. An ineligible offensive player is illegally downfield if:

(a) he moves more than one yard beyond the line of scrimmage without contacting an opponent; or

(b) after losing contact with an opponent within one yard of the line of scrimmage, he advances more than one yard beyond the line of scrimmage; or

(c) after losing contact with an opponent more than one yard beyond the line of scrimmage, he continues to move in any direction.

Penalty: For ineligible offensive player downfield: Loss of five yards from the previous spot.

Article 2   **After Pass Is Thrown.** After the ball leaves the passer's hand, ineligible pass receivers can advance more than one yard beyond the line of scrimmage, or beyond the position reached by their initial charge, provided that they do not block or contact a defensive player, who is more than one yard beyond the line of scrimmage, until the ball is touched by a player of either team. Such prior blocking and/or contact is pass interference if it occurs in the vicinity of where the ball is thrown.

<u>A.R. 8.30</u> Second-and-10 on A30. Center A1 blocks his man and drives him to the A32 where he loses contact. He then moves laterally to his right before the ball is

thrown and completed to eligible end A2 who is downed
on the A45.

Ruling: Ineligible man moved laterally beyond the line
after losing contact. Loss of 5 yards. A's ball second-and-
15 on A25 (8-2-1).

A.R. 8.31 Second-and-10 on A30. Ineligible offensive
tackle A1 charges, driving lineman B1 back from his
line. The pass is completed on the A45.

Ruling: Not ineligible player downfield. A's ball first-
and-10 on A45 (8-2-1).

Section 4	**LEGAL AND ILLEGAL CONTACT WITH ELIGIBLE RECEIVERS**
Article 1	**Legal Contact Within Five Yards.** Within five yards of the line of scrimmage, a defensive player may chuck an eligible receiver in front of him. The defender is allowed to maintain continuous and unbroken contact within the five-yard zone, so long as the receiver has not moved beyond a point that is even with the defender.
Article 2	**Illegal Contact Within Five Yards.** Within the five-yard zone, if the player who receives the snap remains in the pocket with the ball, a defender may not make original contact in the back of a receiver, nor may he maintain contact after the receiver has moved beyond a point that is even with the defender.
Article 3	**Illegal Contact Beyond Five-Yard Zone.** Beyond the five-yard zone, if the player who receives the snap remains in the pocket with the ball, a defender may use his hands or arms only to defend or protect himself against impending contact caused by a receiver. If the receiver attempts to evade the defender, the defender cannot initiate contact that redirects, restricts, or impedes the receiver in any way.

Article 4   **Incidental Contact Beyond Five-Yard Zone.** Beyond the five-yard zone, incidental contact may exist between receiver and defender as long as it does not materially affect or significantly impede the receiver, creating a distinct advantage.

Article 5   **Illegal Cut Block.** It is an illegal cut block if:

(a) an eligible receiver who takes a position more than two yards outside of his own tackle (a flexed receiver) is blocked below the waist; or

(b) an eligible receiver who is lined up on or behind the line of scrimmage and is within two yards of his tackle is blocked below the waist after he crosses the line of scrimmage.

Note: An eligible receiver, whether lined up on or behind the line of scrimmage, who is within two yards of his tackle may be blocked below the waist at or behind the line of scrimmage.

Article 6   **Defensive Holding.** It is defensive holding if a player grasps an eligible offensive player (or his jersey) with his hands, or extends an arm or arms to cut off or encircle him. See 12-1-6.

■ Supplemental Note

(1) Any offensive player who pretends to possess the ball, and/or one to whom a teammate pretends to give the ball, may be tackled providing he is crossing his scrimmage line between the offensive tackles of a normal tight offensive line.

Article 7   **End of Restrictions.** If the quarterback or the receiver of the snap demonstrates no further intention to pass the ball, i.e., hands off or pitches the ball to another back, throws a forward or backward pass, loses possession of the ball by a muff that touches the ground or a fumble, or if he is tackled, the restrictions on the defensive team prohibiting illegal contact, an illegal cut block, or defensive holding against an offensive receiver will end. If the quarterback leaves the pocket area with the ball in his possession, the restrictions on illegal contact and an illegal cut block both end, but the restriction on defensive holding remains in effect.

If a team presents an apparent punting formation, defensive acts that normally constitute illegal contact (chuck beyond five yards, etc.) are permitted, provided that the acts do not constitute defensive holding.

Penalty: For illegal contact or holding by the defense: Loss of five yards and automatic first down.

Penalty: For illegal cut block: Loss of 15 yards and automatic first down.

Section 5   **PASS INTERFERENCE**

Article 1   **Definition.** It is pass interference by either team when any act by a player more than one yard beyond the line of scrimmage significantly hinders the progress of an eligible receiver's opportunity to catch the ball. Pass interference can only occur when a forward pass is thrown from behind the line of scrimmage, regardless of whether the pass is legal or illegal, or whether it crosses the line.

Defensive pass interference rules apply from the time the ball is thrown until the ball is touched. See Article 2 for prohibited acts while the ball is in the air.

Offensive pass interference rules apply from the time the ball is snapped until the ball is touched. See Article 2 for prohibited acts while the ball is in the air and Article 4 for prohibited acts prior to the pass.

Article 2   **Prohibited Acts by both teams while the ball is in the air.** Acts that are pass interference include but are not limited to:

(a) Contact by a player who is not playing the ball that restricts the opponent's opportunity to make the catch.

(b) Playing through the back of an opponent in an attempt to make a play on the ball.

(c) Grabbing an opponent's arm(s) in such a manner that restricts his opportunity to catch a pass.

(d) Extending an arm across the body of an opponent, thus restricting his ability to catch a pass, and regardless of whether the player committing such act is playing the ball.

(e) Cutting off the path of an opponent by making contact with him, without playing the ball.

(f) Hooking an opponent in an attempt to get to the ball in such a manner that it causes the opponent's body to turn prior to the ball arriving.

(g) Initiating contact with an opponent by shoving or pushing off, thus creating a separation in an attempt to catch a pass.

Note: If there is any question whether player contact is incidental, the ruling should be no interference.

Article 3   **Permissible Acts by both teams while the ball is in the air.** Acts that are permissible by a player include but are not limited to:

(a) Incidental contact by an opponent's hands, arms, or body when both players are competing for the ball, or neither player is looking for the ball. If there is any question whether contact is incidental, the ruling shall be no interference.

(b) Inadvertent tangling of feet when both players are playing the ball or neither player is playing the ball.

(c) Contact that would normally be considered pass interference, but the pass is clearly uncatchable by the involved players, except as specified in 8-3-2 and 8-5-4 pertaining to blocking downfield by the offense.

(d) Laying a hand on an opponent that does not restrict him in an attempt to make a play on the ball.

(e) Contact by a player who has gained position on an opponent in an attempt to catch the ball.

Note 1: When the ball is in the air, eligible offensive and defensive receivers have the same right to the path of the ball and are subject to the same restrictions.

Note 2: Acts that do not occur more than one yard beyond the line of scrimmage are not pass interference, but could be defensive holding (see 12-1-6).

Note 3: Whenever a team presents an apparent punting formation, defensive acts that normally constitute pass interference are permitted against the end man on the line of scrimmage, or against an eligible receiver behind the line of scrimmage who is aligned or in motion more than one yard outside the end man on the line, provided that the acts do not constitute illegal holding. Defensive holding, such as tackling a receiver, still can be called and result in a five-yard penalty from the previous spot, if accepted. Offensive pass interference rules still apply.

Article 4   **Other Prohibited Acts By the Offense.** Blocking downfield by an offensive player prior to a pass being thrown is offensive pass interference.

Note: It is also pass interference by the offense to block a defender beyond the line while the pass is in the air, if the block occurs in the vicinity of the player to whom the pass is thrown.

Penalty: Pass interference by the defense: First down for the offensive team at the spot of the foul. If the interference is also a personal foul (12-2), the 15-yard penalty for such a foul is also enforced, either from the spot of the foul (for interference), or from the end of the run if the foul for pass interference is declined. If the interference is behind the defensive goal line, it is first down for the offensive team on the defense's one-yard line, or, if the previous spot was inside the two-yard line, halfway between the previous spot and the goal line.

Penalty: Pass interference by the offense: Loss of 10 yards from the previous spot.

A.R. 8.32 Second-and-10 on A30. On a swing pass from behind the line, a defensive man blocks eligible end A1 on the A32 while the ball is in the air. The pass is incomplete behind the line.
Ruling: Defensive pass interference. It is defensive pass interference regardless of whether the pass crosses the line once the ball is thrown. A's ball first-and-10 on A32.

A.R. 8.33 Second-and-10 on A30. Eligible tight end A1 goes across his line on the snap and blocks defensive player B1 on the A35 before eligible flanker A2 catches it on the A34. Flanker A2 goes to the A45.
Ruling: Offensive pass interference. Can't block beyond the line prior to the ball being touched. A's ball second-and-20 on A20.

A.R. 8.34 Second-and-10 on A30. Eligible offensive player A1 touches the ball on the A45 and the ball goes off his hands. Defensive player B1 then blocks eligible A2 and prevents him from catching the ball on the 50. **Ruling:** Legal block. The ball was touched. No pass interference. A's ball third-and-10 on A30.

A.R. 8.35 Second-and-10 on A30. On a quick pass over the center, defensive player B1 touches the ball on the A35 and it goes high in the air. Defensive player B2 is about to catch the ball when offensive end A1 pushes B2 out of the way and catches the ball and goes to the A45. **Ruling:** Legal play as the ball was touched by the defense. Interference rules ended when defensive player touched the pass. A's ball first-and-10 on A45.

A.R. 8.36 Second-and-10 on A30. Eligible offensive player A1 and B1 both make a bona fide attempt to catch a pass on the A45. There is contact between them and the pass falls incomplete on the A45. **Ruling:** Incomplete pass. Legal play as it was a simultaneous and bona fide attempt by opposing players. A's ball third-and-10 on A30.

A.R. 8.37 Second-and-10 on A30. Tight end A2 blocks B1 on the A35 as the quarterback is looking for an open receiver. A2 then runs to the 50. The quarterback then throws a pass which A2 catches as no one is near him. **Ruling:** Offensive pass interference. A's ball second-and-20 on A20.

A.R. 8.38 Second-and-10 on A30. Defensive player B1, beyond the line, has his back to the ball during a forward pass. He makes no attempt to catch it but waves his arms in close proximity to an eligible opponent on the A45, but there is no contact with receiver. **Ruling:** No foul. Legal action by defender.

A.R. 8.39 Fourth-and-1 on B4. Offensive end A1 pushes a defensive player out of the way in the end zone to catch a legal pass.

Ruling: Loss of 10 yards from previous spot. A's ball fourth-and-11 on B14.

A.R. 8.40 Second-and-10 on B30. A defensive player pushes eligible offensive player A1 out of the way in the end zone and catches a pass. He returns it to the 50.

Ruling: Defensive pass interference in the defensive end zone. A's ball first-and-goal on B1.

A.R. 8.41 Fourth-and-10 on B15. On a fake field goal attempt place-kick holder A1 stands up and throws a pass to eligible end A2 who pushes defensive player B1 out of the way in the end zone to catch the pass there.

Ruling: Offensive pass interference. A's ball fourth-and-20 on B25.

A.R. 8.42 Second-and-10 on A30. A defensive player clips eligible offensive player A1 on the A45 as he is about to catch a pass. The pass falls incomplete on the 50.

Ruling: Interference is also a personal foul and penalize for both. A's ball first-and-10 on B40.

A.R. 8.43 Second-and-10 on A30. During a pass, defensive player B1 grabs the facemask of offensive eligible player A1 on the A35. The ball is thrown to the 50 where defensive B2 interferes with eligible A2. The pass falls incomplete.

Ruling: Additional yardage would have been tacked on if the personal foul (face mask) was the pass interference at the 50 or if the pass had been completed (8-3-3). A's ball first-and-10 on 50.

Section 6   **ENFORCEMENT OF FOULS**

Article 1   **Enforcement Spot.** If there is a foul by either team from the time of the snap until a forward pass thrown from behind the line ends, the penalty is enforced from the previous spot.

Exceptions:

(a) Pass interference by the defense is enforced from the spot of the foul.

(b) If there is a personal foul or unsportsmanlike foul by the defense prior to completion of a forward pass thrown from behind the line, enforcement is pursuant to 8-6-2 below.

(c) If there is a personal foul or unsportsmanlike foul by the offense prior to interception of a forward pass thrown from behind the line, enforcement is pursuant to 8-6-3 below.

(d) It is a safety when the offensive team commits a foul behind its own goal line.

Article 2   **Personal Foul or Unsportsmanlike Foul by Defense Prior to Completion.** When the defense commits a personal foul or unsportsmanlike foul prior to a completion of a legal forward pass thrown from behind the line, the foul will be enforced from the previous spot or the dead-ball spot, whichever is more advantageous to the offense.

Exception: If the passing team is fouled and loses possession after a completion, enforcement is from the previous spot, and the ball will be retained by the passing team after enforcement of the personal foul.

Article 3   **Personal Foul or Unsportsmanlike Foul by Offense Prior to Change of Possession.** When the offense commits a personal foul or unsportsmanlike foul prior to an interception, or the recovery by the defense of a backward pass or fumble, a 15-yard penalty will be enforced from the dead-ball spot.

Exception: If the intercepting or recovering team loses possession after the interception or recovery, enforcement is from the spot where the interception or recovery occurred, and the ball will be retained by the intercepting or recovering team after the enforcement for the personal foul.

Note: When the dead-ball spot is normally a touchback, enforcement is from the 20-yard line.

A.R. 8.44 Third-and-10 on A30. During a run prior to an incomplete pass, offensive player A1 holds a defensive player on the A25.
Ruling: Choice for defense. Fourth-and-10 on A30 or third-and-20 on A20 (from previous spot).

A.R. 8.45 Third-and-10 on A30. During a run prior to an intended pass by quarterback A1, defensive player B1 holds flanker A2 on the A45. Quarterback A1 doesn't throw the ball and is downed on the A20.
Ruling: Enforce from the previous spot. A's ball first-and-10 on A35.

A.R. 8.46 Third-and-10 on A40. Defensive player B1 roughs the passer prior to a pass completion to eligible end A1 on the B45. A1 runs to the B40 where he is downed.
Ruling: Personal foul prior to completion of a legal forward pass. Fifteen-yard penalty enforced from the spot where the ball is dead. A's ball first-and-10 on B25.

A.R. 8.47 Third-and-10 on A40. A defensive player roughs the passer as he throws a short swing pass to back A1 who is downed on the A35. The foul is prior to the completion of the pass.

Ruling: Enforce from the previous spot as the usual penalty on a pass. A's ball first-and-10 on B45.

A.R. 8.48 Third-and-10 on A40. Offensive guard A1 clips defensive player B1 as he tries to reach the passer. B2 intercepts the pass and returns it to the A30.
Ruling: Enforce from the spot where the ball is dead. Personal foul prior to interception. B's ball first-and-10 on A15.

A.R. 8.49 Third-and-10 on A40. Defensive player B1 roughs the passer prior to a completed pass to end A1 on the 50. A1 runs to the B40 where he is tackled, fumbles and the defensive team recovers on the B35.
Ruling: Personal foul prior to completion. Enforce from the previous spot and the ball reverts to the offended team. A's ball first-and-10 on the B45.

A.R. 8.50 Third-and-10 on A30. B1 intercepts forward pass at B30, runs to the B35, fumbles and Team A recovers. Prior to pass, A3 crackbacks on A26.
Ruling: B's ball first-and-10 on B45.

A.R. 8.51 Third-and-10 on A40. Defensive player B1 roughs the passer prior to a completion to eligible end A1 on the B40. A1 goes for a score.
Ruling: Touchdown. Loss of 15 on the kickoff. Kick off on A45. See 14-1-14.

A.R. 8.52 Second-and-10 on A30. During a forward pass the ball goes off eligible end A1's fingers and flanker A2 catches it on the B40. The defensive team was offside.
Ruling: A's ball first-and-10 on B40.

A.R. 8.53 Second-and-10 on A30. A forward pass is caught by ineligible tackle on A28. B1 was offside.
Ruling: Penalties offset. Second-and-10 on A30.

A.R. 8.54 Second-and-10 on A30. A forward pass is caught by ineligible A2 beyond the line. Prior to or during the pass, defensive player B1 strikes A1.
Ruling: Disqualify B1. A's ball first-and-10 on A45.

Section 7 **BACKWARD PASS AND FUMBLE**

Article 1 **Backward Pass.** A runner may throw a backward pass at any time (3-22-4). Players of either team may advance after catching a backward pass, or recovering a backward pass after it touches the ground.

Exception: See actions to conserve time (4-7-1).

Note: A direct snap from center to a player in the backfield, a muffed hand-to-hand snap, or a snap that is untouched by a player who is in position to receive a hand-to-hand snap are backward passes, and the ball remains alive.

A.R. 8.55 Fourth-and-10 on A40. A high snap from center glances off the kicker's hands as he muffs the ball on the A28. The ball rolls to the A25. A defensive player picks it up and goes for a score.
Ruling: Touchdown. (8-4-1-Note)

A.R. 8.56 A's ball fourth-and-10 on B20. Direct snap from center on an attempted field goal glances off place-kick holder's hands at the B27. Field goal kicker recovers the ball at B30 and *runs for a touchdown.*
Ruling: Legal touchdown. See 8-4-1-Note.

Article 2 **Backward Pass Out of Bounds.** If a backward pass goes out of bounds between the goal lines, the ball is dead (7-5-5), and it is next put in play at the inbounds spot. Rule 11 governs if a backward pass is declared dead behind the goal line.

Article 3 **Fumble.** A fumble is any act, other than a pass or kick, which results in a loss of player possession.

Exception: If a runner intentionally fumbles forward, it is a forward pass (3-22-2-a and Note 4).

Item 1: Recovery and Advance. Any player of either team may recover or catch a fumble and advance, either before or after the ball strikes the ground.

Exceptions:

(a) Fourth-down fumble. See 8-7-5 below.

(b) Fumble after two-minute warning. See 8-7-6 below.

Item 2: Legal Recovery. For a legal recovery of a fumble, see Rule 3, Section 2, Article 7. See 7-5-6-a for fumble out of bounds and 11-5-1-Exc. 2 for a fumble in the end zone following intercepting momentum.

Item 3: Out of Bounds. For fumbles forward out of bounds or unrecovered in the field of play or in the end zone, see 7-5-6.

Article 4 **Handing Ball Forward.** No player may hand the ball forward except to an eligible receiver who is behind the line of scrimmage.

(a) Loss of player possession by unsuccessful execution of attempted handing is a fumble charged to the player that last had possession.

(b) A muffed handoff (legal or illegal) is a fumble, and the ball remains alive.

Penalty: For handing the ball forward beyond the line of scrimmage or not from scrimmage: Five yards and loss of down from the spot of the foul.

Penalty: For handing the ball forward to an ineligible receiver behind the line of scrimmage: Loss of five yards.

Article 5 **Fourth Down Fumble.** If a fourth-down fumble occurs during a play from scrimmage:

(a) The ball may be advanced by any member of the defensive team.

(b) The player who fumbled is the only Team A player permitted to recover and advance the ball.

(c) If the recovery or catch is by a teammate of the player who fumbled, the ball is dead, and the spot of the next snap is the spot of the fumble, or the spot of the recovery if the spot of the recovery is behind the spot of the fumble. See 8-4-3.

Note 1: After a change of possession has occurred, the restrictions in (b) and (c) are no longer in effect for the remainder of the down.

Note 2: The restrictions in (b) and (c) are applicable during the Try throughout the game.

Article 6   **Fumble After Two-Minute Warning.** If a fumble by either team occurs after the two-minute warning:

(a) The ball may be advanced by any opponent.

(b) The player who fumbled is the only player of his team who is permitted to recover and advance the ball.

(c) If the recovery or catch is by a teammate of the player who fumbled, the ball is dead, and the spot of the next snap is the spot of the fumble, or the spot of the recovery if the spot of the recovery is behind the spot of the fumble.

A.R. 8.57 Second-and-10 on B14. On last play of game Team A is behind by 4 points. Quarterback A1 falls back to pass, fumbles, and ball eventually winds up in B's end zone. A2 falls on it.
Ruling: No score. Game over. See 8-4-2, S.N.

A.R. 8.58 Fourth-and-four on B9. Offensive player A1 fumbles (forward unintentionally) on the B9. A1 recovers and goes to the B4.
Ruling: Legal advance as the fumbling player recovered. A's ball first-and-goal on B4.

A.R. 8.59 Fourth-and-four on B9. Offensive player A1 fumbles on the B9 (forward unintentionally). His teammate A2 recovers on the B7 and goes to the B4.
Ruling: Player other than the fumbling player recovered. The spot of the snap is the spot of the fumble (B9). B's ball first-and-10 on B9.

A.R. 8.60 Fourth-and-four on B9. Offensive player A1 fumbles on the B9 and A2 recovers on the B12 and goes to the B4.
Ruling: Other player than the fumbler recovered and spot of next snap is the spot of recovery as it is behind the spot of the fumble. B's ball first-and-10 on B12.

A.R. 8.61 Fourth-and-four on B9. Offensive player A1 fumbles on the B9. Defensive player B1 touches the ball and then offensive player A2 recovers on the B7.
Ruling: Ball is returned to spot of fumble (B9). B's ball first-and-10 on B9.

A.R. 8.62 Fourth-and-four on B9. A1 fumbles on the B9 and the ball rolls out of bounds on the B4 without any player touching it.
Ruling: The ball is next put in play at the spot of the fumble. B's ball first-and-10 on B9.

Article 7   **Enforcement Spot During a Backward Pass or Fumble.** When a foul occurs during a backward pass or fumble, the basic spot of enforcement is the spot of the backward pass or fumble.

Exceptions:

(a) Behind the Line. When the spot of the backward pass or fumble is behind the line (including in A's end zone), if either team fouls, the spot of enforcement is the previous spot, even if B's foul is in A's end zone. If Team A fouls in its own end zone during a backward pass or fumble, the enforcement of the penalty results in a safety.

(b) Beyond the Line. When the spot of the backward pass or fumble is beyond the line, and the spot of an offensive foul is behind the spot of the backward pass or fumble:

   (i) If the foul occurs beyond the line of scrimmage, the spot of enforcement is the spot of the foul; or

   (ii) If the foul occurs behind the line of scrimmage, the spot of enforcement is the previous spot; or

   (iii) If the spot of the foul is in A's end zone, enforcement of the foul results in a safety.

(c) For enforcement when the offense commits a personal foul or unsportsmanlike foul prior to the recovery by the defense of a backward pass or fumble, see Section 6, Article 3 above.

A.R. 8.63 First-and-10 on A40. Runner A1 advances to the 50 where he passes backward. During the backward pass A2 holds on the A45. The ball goes out of bounds on the A48.
Ruling: Enforcement is from the spot of the foul as it is behind the basic spot (14-1-5-d). A's ball first-and-15 on A35.

A.R. 8.64 Fourth-and-15 on A8. A punt is blocked and the ball is in the end zone when defensive player B1 pushes A1 out of the way to allow his teammate B2 to recover the ball in the end zone.
Ruling: The spot of enforcement is the previous spot as the foul by the defense occurred behind this line. A's ball first-and-10 on A13.

A.R. 8.65 Second-and-10 on B30. Quarterback A1 fumbles on the B32. A defensive player bats the loose ball in flight to the B40 where A1 recovers.

Ruling: The enforcement spot is the previous spot as the foul is behind the line. Illegal bat (12-1-8). A's ball first-and-10 on B20.

A.R. 8.66 Second-and-10 on B30. Quarterback A1 passes backward and a defensive player bats the pass in flight. The ball goes to the B40 where A1 recovers. **Ruling:** Legal bat (12-1-8-Exc.). A's ball third-and-20 on B40.

A.R. 8.67 Second-and-10 on B30. A backward pass or fumble hits the ground on the B35 and a defensive player bats the ball to the B40 where he recovers. **Ruling:** Illegal bat of a loose ball. Enforcement is from the previous spot as it is behind the line. A's ball first-and-10 on B20.

A.R. 8.68 B1 intercepts a forward pass in his end zone and advances to his 2 yard line where he fumbles. B1 recovers. During the fumble B2 fouls:

a) in his end zone.
   Ruling: Safety. Enforcement is from the spot of the foul as it is not from scrimmage. See 11-4-2 and 14-1-11-h.

b) on his 5-yard line.
   Ruling: B's ball first-and-10 on B1. Enforcement is from the spot of the fumble.

A.R. 8.69 Third-and-15 on B30. B1 intercepts a pass in the end zone and runs it out to the B20 where he throws a backward pass which hits the ground on the B15. A1 recovers on the ground and scores. **Ruling:** Legal recovery and advance by A1. Touchdown Team A (8-4-1-b).

A.R. 8.70 A backward pass or fumble by offensive Team A on its 4-yard line comes to rest on the 2-yard line. Offensive player A1 blocks B1 into the ball and causes it to cross the goal line.

a) A2 recovers in the end zone.
    Ruling: Safety if A2 is downed in the end zone. May advance if he can (3-14-3-Note).
b) B2 recovers in the end-zone.
    Ruling: Touchdown.

A.R. 8.71 Second-and-10 on B30. A ball is handed forward by quarterback to eligible receiver A2 who is behind his line. Receiver A2 muffs ball and defensive player B recovers on the B35 and goes to the 50.
Ruling: Legal advance. It is not a forward pass (3-21-2-Exc.), and it is treated as a fumble. B's ball first-and-10 on 50.

A.R. 8.72 Second-and-10 on B30. A ball is handed backward (no daylight) to ineligible receiver A1 on the B35. A1 muffs the ball and B1 recovers and goes to the 50.
Ruling: Legal recovery. A ball which is handed backward from one player to another (no daylight) and is dropped, shall be treated as a fumble. Either team may recover and advance. B's ball first-and-10 on 50.

Scrimmage

Kick

Rule 9

Scrimmage Kick

Section 1 **KICK FROM SCRIMMAGE**

Article 1 Team A may attempt a punt, drop kick, or placekick
from behind the line of scrimmage.

**Penalty: For a punt, drop kick, or placekick that is
kicked from beyond the line of scrimmage or not from
scrimmage: Loss of 10 yards from the spot of the kick.**

Note 1: This is not considered illegally kicking the ball.

*Note 2: The penalty for a punt, drop kick, or placekick
from beyond the line is to be enforced from the spot where
the ball is punted or kicked when the player's entire body
and the ball are beyond the line of scrimmage. This includes
either when the player is airborne or touching the ground.*

Article 2 During a kick from scrimmage, only the end men (eligible receivers) on the line of scrimmage at the time of the
snap, or an eligible receiver who is aligned or in motion
behind the line and is more than one yard outside the
end man, are permitted to advance more than one yard
beyond the line before the ball is kicked.

**Penalty: For advancing more than one yard beyond the
line of scrimmage before the ball is kicked: Loss of five
yards.**

Article 3 The following blocking rules apply during a scrimmage
kick down:

(a) All players on the receiving team are prohibited from
blocking below the waist during a down in which
there is a scrimmage kick, except for players on the
line of scrimmage who are lined up on or inside the
normal tight end position. Immediately at the snap,
such players are permitted to block low.

After the ball has been kicked, all players on the kicking team are prohibited from blocking below the waist for the remainder of the down.

(b) Prior to the ball being kicked, the kicking team is subject to the blocking restrictions applicable to the offense, and the receiving team is subject to the blocking restrictions applicable to the defense, except that a kicking team player may use his hands to ward off, push, or pull aside a receiver who is legally or illegally attempting to obstruct his attempt to proceed downfield.

(c) After the ball is kicked and goes beyond the line of scrimmage, and until the kick ends (either team secures possession of the ball, or the ball is dead by rule), the kicking team is subject to the blocking restrictions of the defense, and the receiving team is subject to the blocking restrictions of the offense. (For the exception prohibiting a block in the back by the kicking team while the ball is in flight, see 12-1-4-Note). After the kick ends, both teams are subject to the normal restrictions applicable to offense and defense.

Exception: If the ball goes beyond the line of scrimmage and returns behind the line untouched by the receiving team beyond the line, the blocking restrictions do not change, and the kicking team continues to be subject to the blocking restrictions of the offense and the receiving team to the blocking restrictions of the defense.

(d) After the ball has been kicked, and until the receiving team establishes possession, the yardage for penalties by either team should be enforced as for offensive fouls, unless the ball does not go beyond the line of scrimmage, or the ball goes beyond the line and returns behind the line untouched by the receiving team beyond the line.

Article 4   During a punt that crosses the line of scrimmage, and prior to a change of possession, it is a foul if a kicking team player goes out of bounds voluntarily (without being contacted) prior to the end of the kick.

Penalty: Loss of five yards.

Section 2   **TOUCHING A SCRIMMAGE KICK**

Article 1   Any touching of the ball behind the line of scrimmage by a kicking team player is legal, even if the ball has crossed the line and returns behind the line.

Article 2   "First touching" is when a player of the kicking team touches a scrimmage kick that is beyond the line of scrimmage before it has been touched by a player of the receiving team beyond the line. If the ball is first touched by a player of the kicking team, it remains in play. First touching is a violation, and the receivers shall have the option of taking possession of the ball at the spot of first touching, provided no penalty is accepted on the play, or at the spot where the ball is dead. First touching does not offset a foul by the receivers.

Note: If the receiving team gains possession, subsequently loses possession, and fouls after the kicking team gains possession, the spot of first touching is disregarded, and the kicking team retains possession. See Rule 14, Section 3, Article 1, Exception 5.

Item 1: A Team B player is deemed not to have touched a kick if such touching occurs in the immediate vicinity of the line in an attempt to block the kick.

Item 2: If a player of the kicking team touches the goal line with any part of his body while touching the ball, the ball is dead, and the result of the play is a touchback.

Note: The spot of first touching is normally the yard line at which the ball is at when touched. If the first touching occurs while the ball is in the air above or beyond the goal line, and prior to the ball touching the goal line or the ground beyond the goal line, the spot of first touching is deemed to be the spot from which the touching player left the field of play, but in no event inside the receiving team's one-yard line.

Article 3 A player of the kicking team, who has been out of bounds, may not touch or recover a scrimmage kick beyond the line of scrimmage until it has been touched by a kicking team player who has not been out of bounds, or until it has been touched by a player of the receiving team beyond the line.

Note: If a player touches or recovers the ball before he has re-established himself inbounds, the ball is out-of-bounds at the spot of the touch, and there is no foul.

Penalty: For illegal touching of a scrimmage kick: Loss of five yards. If the illegal touching is inside the receiver's five-yard line, in addition to the other specified options, the receiving team may elect to take a touchback.

Article 4 There is no distinction between a player touching a ball or being touched by it, but a player is not considered to have touched the ball if he is blocked into it by an opponent, provided he is in a passive position and not blocking. A player who is engaged with and blocking his opponent when he contacts the ball is deemed to have touched the ball.

Section 3 CATCH OR RECOVERY OF A SCRIMMAGE KICK

Article 1 When a scrimmage kick is caught or recovered by the kicking team behind the line of scrimmage, the kicking team may **advance**, even if the ball has crossed the line and returned behind the line (see 3-28-2, S.N. 2).

Note: If the kicking team catches or recovers a kick behind the line during a try-kick, the ball is dead as soon as it is evident that the kick has failed, and no advance is permitted (11-3-2).

Item 1: Same Series of Downs. If the ball has returned behind the line untouched by the receiving team beyond the line, and the kicking team catches or recovers the ball, the existing series of downs continues unless the kicking team advances the ball to the line to gain, in which case there is a new series of downs.

Item 2: New Series of Downs. If the ball has returned behind the line after being touched by the receiving team beyond the line, and the kicking team catches or recovers the ball, by rule there has been a change of possession, and the kicking team will be awarded a new series of downs.

Article 2 When the kickers catch or recover a kick beyond the line of scrimmage, the ball is **dead** at the spot of recovery, even if a member of the receiving team has first touched the ball.

Item 1: Legal Catch or Recovery. If the receiving team touches the ball beyond the line, a subsequent catch or recovery by the kicking team is legal, but the ball is dead. In the event of such a catch or recovery, it is first-and-10 for the kickers, or if the ball is caught or recovered by the kickers in the receiver's end zone, it is a touchdown for the kickers. See 7-1-1-d.

Item 2: Illegal Catch or Recovery. If the kickers catch or recover a kick beyond the line that has not been touched beyond the line by the receiving team, the ball is dead, and it is first-and-10 for the receivers at the spot of catch or recovery (see 11-4-2 for missed goals). If a kick from behind the line is touched by the receiving team behind the line, such touching does not make the kicking team eligible to catch or recover the kick beyond the line.

Item 3: If a player of the kicking team illegally catches or recovers a scrimmage kick, other than a field goal attempt from beyond the 20-yard line, and carries the ball across the goal line, or touches the goal line with any part of his body while in possession of the ball, the ball is dead, and the result of the play is a touchback. For a missed field goal from beyond the 20-yard line, see 11-4-2.

Article 3   If the receivers catch or recover any kick, they may **advance**. For fair catch exception, see 10-2-3. For exception for a ball that has crossed the goal line, see Section 4.

Article 4   When a legal kick is simultaneously caught or recovered anywhere by two eligible opposing players, or if the ball is lying on the field of play with no player attempting to recover it, it is awarded to the receivers. See 7-4-2.

Section 4   **BALL CROSSES GOAL LINE, TOUCHES GOAL POSTS, OUT OF BOUNDS, DEAD IN FIELD OF PLAY**

Article 1   If a scrimmage kick crosses the receiver's goal line from the impetus of the kick, the following shall apply:

(a) If the ball has not been touched by a player of the receiving team beyond the line of scrimmage, it is dead immediately, and the result of the play is a touchback, when: (1) it touches the ground on or behind the receiver's goal line, (2) it touches a player of the kicking team who is touching the ground on or behind the receiver's goal line, or (3) it touches a player of the kicking team who has touched the ground on or behind the receiver's goal line and has not re-established himself in the field of play. See Rule 11 for options for missed field goals beyond the 20-yard line.

(b) If the receivers catch the ball in the end zone, or recover it in the end zone after touching it in the field of play or the end zone, they may advance.

(c) If the kickers catch or recover the ball in the end zone after the receivers first touch the ball in the field of play or the end zone, it is a touchdown for the kickers.

(d) If there is a spot of first touching by the kickers outside the receivers' 20-yard line, the receiving team has the option to take possession of the ball at the spot of the first touching.

(e) If the scrimmage kick is a punt, and the ball goes out of bounds in the field of play after being touched by a receiver in the end zone or in the field of play, it is the receiving team's ball at the out-of-bounds spot.

Article 2   If a missed field goal or try, or a punt, has touched the receiver's goal post, uprights, or crossbar, the ball is dead in the receiver's end zone, and all customary rules pertaining to punts, missed field goals, and trys apply.

Article 3   If a scrimmage kick touches the kickers' goal post, uprights, or crossbar, the ball is dead, and it is a safety. See 11-5-1.

Article 4   If a scrimmage kick goes out of bounds between the goal lines or is lying in the field of play with no player attempting to recover it, it is the receiver's ball at the dead-ball spot, unless the special rules for missed field goals in 11-4-2 apply.

Section 5   SPOTS OF ENFORCEMENT

Article 1   If there is a foul from the time of the snap until a legal scrimmage kick ends, enforcement is from the previous spot. This includes a foul during a run prior to a legal kick (14-1-13-S.N. 1), and running into or roughing the kicker (12-2-6). If the offensive team commits a foul in its own end zone, it is a safety.

Exception 1: Unless the kick is a missed field-goal attempt, if there is a foul by the kicking team, the receiving team will have the option of taking the penalty at the previous spot and replaying the down, or adding the penalty yardage on to the dead-ball spot.

Note 1: The dead-ball spot for kicks that result in a touchback is the 20-yard line.

Note 2: If there is an illegal touch inside the five-yard line, the receiving team also has the option of accepting a touchback.

Exception 2: Fair catch interference, interference with the opportunity to make a catch, an invalid fair catch signal, or a personal foul (blocking) after a fair catch signal are enforced from the spot of the foul.

Exception 3: If the receiving team commits a foul after the ball has been kicked and has gone beyond the line of scrimmage, and the receivers possess and thereafter keep the ball throughout the remainder of the down, the penalty for their infraction will be ruled as a foul after possession (post-possession) and shall be assessed from whichever of the following is least advantageous to them:

(a) The spot where possession is gained;

(b) The spot where the ball becomes dead; or

(c) The spot of the foul.

Exception 4: If the receiving team commits a foul after the ball has been kicked and has gone beyond the line of scrimmage, and there is a first touch by the kicking team, if the receiving team subsequently loses possession, the ball reverts to the receiving team, and its penalty shall be assessed from whichever is least advantageous to them:

(a) The spot where possession was gained by the receiving team; or

(b) The spot of the foul.

Note: The spot of the first touch is not used.

Opportunity to Catch a Kick, Fair Catch

Rule 10

Opportunity to Catch a Kick, Fair Catch

Section 1 **OPPORTUNITY TO CATCH A KICK**

Article 1 During a scrimmage kick that crosses the line of scrimmage, or during a free kick, members of the kicking team are prohibited from interfering with any receiver making an attempt to catch the airborne kick, or from obstructing or hindering his path to the airborne kick, and regardless of whether any signal was given.

Item 1: Contact with Receiver. It is interference if a player of the kicking team contacts the receiver, or causes a passive player of either team to contact the receiver, before or simultaneous to his touching the ball.

Item 2: Right of Way. A receiver who is moving toward a kicked ball that is in flight has the right of way. If opponents obstruct his path to the ball, or cause a passive player of either team to obstruct his path, it is interference, even if there is no contact, or if he catches the ball in spite of the interference, and regardless of whether any signal was given.

Penalties:

(a) For interference with the opportunity to make a catch when a prior signal has not been made: Loss of 15 yards from the spot of the foul, and the offended team is entitled to put the ball in play by a snap from scrimmage. See 4-8-2-g.

(b) For interfering with a fair catch after a signal: Loss of 15 yards from the spot of the foul. A fair catch is awarded even if the ball is not caught. See Section 2, Article 4.

Section 2 FAIR CATCH

Article 1 A Fair Catch is an unhindered catch of an airborne scrimmage kick that has crossed the line of scrimmage, or of an airborne free kick, by a player of the receiving team who has given a valid fair catch signal.

Article 2 **Item 1: Valid Fair-Catch Signal.** A fair-catch signal is valid if it is made while the kick is in flight by a player who fully extends one arm above his helmet and waves it from side to side. A receiver is permitted to legally raise his hand(s) to his helmet to shield his eyes from the sun, but is not permitted to raise them above his helmet except to signal for a fair catch.

Item 2: Invalid Fair-Catch Signal. If a player raises his hand(s) above his shoulder(s) in any other manner, it is an invalid fair-catch signal. If there is an invalid fair-catch signal, the ball is dead when caught or recovered by any player of the receiving team, but it is not a fair catch. (The ball is not dead if it touches an opponent before or after it strikes the ground. See Article 3b).

Note: A fair-catch signal given behind the line of scrimmage on a scrimmage kick is ignored and is neither valid nor invalid.

Penalty: For an invalid fair-catch signal: Loss of five yards from the spot of the signal.

Item 3: Muff. After a valid fair-catch signal, the opportunity to catch a kick does not end if the ball is muffed. The player who signaled for a fair catch must have a reasonable opportunity to catch the muffed ball before it hits the ground without interference by members of the kicking team, and regardless of whether the ball strikes another player or an official.

Penalty: For interference with the opportunity to make a fair catch after a muff: A fair catch is awarded at the spot of the interference even if the ball is not caught.

Item 4: Intentional Muff. An intentional muff forward prior to a catch in order to gain ground is an illegal bat (see 12-1-8).

Item 5: Illegal Block. Until the ball touches a teammate or an opponent, a player who makes a valid or invalid fair-catch signal is prohibited from blocking or initiating contact with a player of the kicking team.

Penalty: For an illegal block after a fair-catch signal: Loss of 15 yards from the spot of the foul.

Article 3 (a) If a player of the receiving team makes a valid fair-catch signal, and the ball is not touched by a player of the kicking team, the following apply:

(1) If he catches the ball, it is dead immediately, and it is a fair catch. If he muffs the ball, but catches it before it touches the ground, it is also a fair catch. After a fair catch, the ball is next put in play by the receiving team at the dead-ball spot (or at the succeeding spot after enforcement of any applicable penalties). See Article 4.

(2) If he recovers the ball after it strikes the ground, it is dead immediately, but it is not a fair catch.

(3) If the ball is caught or recovered by a teammate who did not make a valid fair-catch signal, the ball is dead immediately, but it is not a fair catch. The ball will next be put in play by a snap by the receiving team at the dead-ball spot (or at the succeeding spot after enforcement of any applicable penalties).

(b) If the ball touches a player of the kicking team, before or after it strikes the ground, any player of the receiving team may catch or recover it and advance. If a player of the receiving team who has given a valid fair-catch signal catches the ball before it hits the ground and elects not to advance the ball, it is a fair catch.

(c) After a receiver has made a fair catch, an opponent is prohibited from blocking or tackling him, or causing a passive player of either team to contact him. Incidental contact is not a foul.

Penalty: For illegal contact with a player who has made a fair catch: Loss of 15 yards from the dead-ball spot and disqualification if flagrant (snap or free kick). See 6-1-3 Note.

Article 4 After a fair catch is made, or is awarded as the result of fair catch interference, the receiving team has the option of putting the ball in play by either:

(a) a fair-catch kick (drop kick or placekick without a tee) from the spot of the catch (or the succeeding spot after enforcement of any applicable penalties) (3-9-1 and 11-4-3), or

(b) a snap from the spot of the catch (or the succeeding spot after enforcement of any applicable penalties).

Note: A receiver may make or be awarded a fair catch in his end zone. If there is fair-catch interference or illegal contact with the receiver after he has made a fair catch, the 15 yard penalty is enforced from the receiver's 20 yard line, and the option for a fair-catch kick is awarded.

Article 5 If time expires during a play in which a player has signaled for a fair catch, the following shall apply:

(a) If the player makes a fair catch, the receiving team may elect to extend the period with a fair-catch kick, but does not have the option to extend the period by a snap from scrimmage.

      (b) If the kicking team interferes with a receiver who has signaled for a fair catch, the receiving team will be awarded a 15-yard penalty and the option to extend the period by attempting a fair-catch kick or by a snap from scrimmage.

Scoring

Rule 11

Scoring

Section 1   **VALUE OF SCORES**

Article 1   **Winning Team.** The team that scores the greater number of points during the entire game is the winner.

Note: If a team forfeits a game, the opponent will be declared the winner by a score of 2-0, but the points will not be added to the winning team's record for purposes of offensive production or tie-breakers.

Article 2   **Types of Scoring Plays.** Points are scored as follows:
(a) Touchdown: 6 points;
(b) Field Goal: 3 points;
(c) Safety: 2 points;
(d) Successful Try after touchdown: 1 point (Field Goal or Safety) or 2 points (Touchdown)

Section 2   **TOUCHDOWN**

Article 1   **Touchdown Plays.** A touchdown is scored when:

(a) the ball is on, above, or behind the plane of the opponents' goal line and is in possession of a runner who has advanced from the field of play; or

(b) a ball in possession of an airborne runner is on, above, or behind the plane of the goal line, and some part of the ball passed over or inside the pylon; or

(c) a ball in player possession touches the pylon, provided that, after contact by an opponent, no part of the player's body, except his hands or feet, struck the ground before the ball touched the pylon; or

(d) any player who is legally inbounds catches or recovers a loose ball (3-2-3) that is on, above, or behind the opponent's goal line; or

(e) the Referee awards a touchdown to a team that has been denied one by a palpably unfair act.

■ Supplemental Notes

(1) The ball is automatically dead when it is in legal possession of a player and is on, above, or behind the opponent's goal line.

(2) If the player is attempting to catch a pass, the ball is not dead, and a touchdown is not scored, until the receiver completes the catch. See Rule 3, Section 2, Article 7.

A.R. 11.1 Third-and-goal on B2. Runner A1 goes to the goal line with the ball over the plane of the goal line. He is tackled and fumbles and the defensive team recovers in the end zone.
Ruling: Touchdown. The ball is automatically dead at the instant of legal player possession on the opponent's goal line.

A.R. 11.2 Second-and-10 on B18. Runner A1 takes handoff and runs down the sideline toward the goal line with the ball in his outside arm. He crosses the goal line plane standing with the ball to the outside of the pylon.
Ruling: Touchdown. Part of the ball crossing over or inside the pylon only applies to an airborne runner who lands out of bounds.

Section 3   TRY

Article 1 **General Rules.** After a touchdown, the scoring team is awarded a Try in an attempt to score one or two additional points during one scrimmage down.

The Try begins when the Referee sounds his whistle for play to start. The spot of the snap shall be:

(a) anywhere on or between the inbounds lines, and

(b) two yards from the defensive team's goal line.

Note 1: All general rules for fourth-down fumbles apply to the Try (See 8-7-5).

Note 2: The Game Clock will not run during the Try.

Note 3: If the ball has been declared ready for play by the Referee, and the offensive team wants to change the location of the ball, they can do so by calling a timeout.

Note 4: See 7-2-2 for restriction applicable to Team B formation at the snap.

Note 5: See 16-1-1 for exception when a touchdown is scored in an overtime period.

Article 2:   **Results of a Try.** During a Try, the following shall apply:

(a) If a kick results in a field goal by the offense, one point is awarded. An artificial or manufactured tee shall not be permitted to assist in the execution of a Try-kick. (The conditions of 11-4-1 must be met.) The ball is dead as soon as it becomes evident that the kick has failed.

(b) If a Try results in a touchdown by the offense, two points are awarded. If a touchdown is not scored, the Try is over at the end of the play.

(c) If the defense gains possession, the ball is dead immediately. The defensive team cannot score during a Try.

(d) If there is no kick, and the Try results in what would ordinarily be a safety against the defense, one point is awarded to the offensive team.

(e) If any play results in a touchback, the Try is unsuccessful, and there shall be no replay.

A.R. 11.3 An attempted Try-kick is blocked. Offensive A1 recovers behind the line and advances across the goal line or recovers in defensive's end zone.
Ruling: No score in either case. The ball is dead as soon as its failure as a kick to score a Try is evident.

A.R. 11.4 During a Try, placekick holder A1 fumbles. B1 kicks, bats, or muffs the loose ball (new impetus) on his 2 and it goes out of bounds behind the goal line.
Ruling: Ordinarily a safety (11-4-1). Award one point.

Article 3 **Fouls Committed During Try**

Item 1: Fouls Before the Signal. If there is a foul by either team after a touchdown and before the ready-for-play signal, it is enforced on the next kickoff.

A.R. 11.5 Offensive player A1 clips after runner A2 had scored a touchdown.
Ruling: Penalty is enforced from the succeeding spot which is the spot of the next kickoff. Spot of ball for Try is from 2 or more yards from B's goal line. Penalty is not enforced on Try.

Item 2: Fouls Before the Snap. If there is a foul by the offense which causes a play to be whistled dead prior to the snap, it shall be treated the same as if it had occurred prior to a scrimmage play. The whistle shall be blown immediately. (See 7-2-3 and 7-3-4). If a foul by the defense prevents the attempt of a Try, the offensive team has the option to have the distance penalty assessed on the next Try or on the ensuing kickoff.

Item 3: Fouls by Team A. The following applies if there is a foul by Team A:

(a) If there is a foul by the offense during a successful Try, after the penalty the Try shall be repeated, unless the penalty for the foul results in a loss of down.

(b) If the penalty for a foul results in a loss of down, the Try is unsuccessful, and there shall be no replay.

Item 4: Fouls by Team B. The following applies if there is a foul by Team B:

(a) If the foul results in a safety, the offensive team is awarded one point.

(b) If the attempted Try is unsuccessful, the offensive team may accept or decline the distance penalty before the down is replayed.

(c) If the attempted Try is successful, all fouls committed by the defense will result in the distance penalty being assessed on the ensuing kickoff, unless the offensive team chooses to attempt a retry after enforcement of the penalty. See A.R. 14.27.

Note: If the foul is for defensive pass interference, and it is declined, no distance penalty is enforced on the kickoff.

Item 5: Fouls by Both Teams. If there are fouls by both teams during a Try, the Try must be replayed (14-3-1). Normal enforcement rules for double fouls apply.

Item 6: Fouls After a Try. If there is a foul by either team after a Try, it is enforced on the succeeding kickoff. If there are fouls by both teams, normal enforcement rules apply.

A.R. 11.6 During a Try, runner A1 is downed on B's 2 in a side zone. During the run, B1 commits a personal foul. **Ruling:** Replay from the previous spot or from the spot after enforcement.

A.R. 11.7 During a Try which is unsuccessful, defensive B1 is offside.
Ruling: Replay at previous spot or one-yard line.

A.R. 11.8 During a Try which is successful, defensive B1 is offside.

Ruling: Try good and loss of yardage on kickoff against Team B, or retry from B1-yard line.

Article 4 **Kickoff After Try.** After a Try, the team on defense during the Try shall receive the kickoff (6-1-1-a).

Section 4 **FIELD GOAL**

Article 1 **Successful Field Goal.** A field goal is scored when all of the following conditions are met:

(a) The kick must be a placekick or dropkick made by the offense from behind the line of scrimmage or from the spot of a fair catch (fair-catch kick). If a fair catch is made or awarded outside the inbounds line, the spot of the kick is the nearest inbounds line.

(b) After the ball is kicked, it must not touch the ground or any player of the offensive team before it passes through the goal.

(c) The entire ball must pass through the vertical plane of the goal, which is the area above the cross-bar and between the uprights or, if above the uprights, between their outside edges of the uprights. If the ball passes through the goal, and returns through the goal without striking the ground or some object or person beyond the goal, the attempt is unsuccessful

Note. See 7-2-2 for restriction applicable to Team B formation at the snap.

Article 2 **Missed Field Goals.** If there is a missed field-goal attempt, and the ball has not been touched by the receivers beyond the line in the field of play, the following shall apply:

(a) If the spot of the kick was inside the receiver's 20-yard line, it is the receivers' ball at the 20-yard line or

---

(b) If the spot of the kick was from the receiver's 20-yard line or beyond the receiver's 20-yard line, it is the receiver's ball at the spot of the kick.

Note: These options apply only if the ball has been beyond the line.

Exception 1: If there is a missed field-goal attempt and the ball is touched by the receivers beyond the line of scrimmage in the field of play, all general rules for a kick from scrimmage will apply, and the special rules pertaining to field goals in (a) and (b) are not applicable. If a foul occurs during the missed field-goal attempt, Rule 9-5-1 governs.

Exception 2: If a field-goal attempt from anywhere on the field is blocked, and the ball has not been beyond the line, general rules for scrimmage kicks apply, and the special rules pertaining to field goals in (a) and (b) are not applicable.

Exception 3: If the ball has gone beyond the line and returns behind the line untouched by Team B beyond the line, and either team recovers and attempts to advance the ball, all special rules for missed field goals in (a) and (b) are no longer applicable, and general rules for scrimmage kicks apply. If either team recovers and does not attempt to advance the ball, Team B has the option to take the ball at the dead-ball spot or the spot of the kick.

Note: If the ball has not been touched by the receivers beyond the line in the field of play and goes out of bounds in the field of play after being touched by a receiver in the end zone, it is the receiving team's option to take the ball at the spot of the kick or the receiving team's 20-yard line.

■ Supplemental Notes

(1) If the receivers do not touch the ball beyond the line of scrimmage in the field of play or in the end zone, and the ball bounces back into the field of play after it touches the ground on or behind the receiver's goal line, it is the receivers' ball at the spot of the kick. If the attempt was from inside the 20-yard line, it is a touchback. The ball is dead as soon as it touches the ground in the end zone.

(2) If the ball goes out of bounds after it is first touched by the receivers beyond the line of scrimmage in the field of play, it is the receivers' ball at the out-of-bounds spot.

(3) If the receivers first touch the ball beyond the line of scrimmage in the field of play or in the end zone, and the kickers recover, the ball belongs to the kickers at the spot of recovery. If the recovery is in the end zone, it is a touchdown.

(4) If the receivers first touch the ball beyond the line of scrimmage in the field of play, and without any new impetus the ball rolls into the end zone where it is declared dead in the possession of the receivers, it is a touchback.

A.R. 11.9 Fourth-and-10 on B35. On a field goal attempt, the ball is kicked from the B42 and is wide and goes over the end line.
Ruling: B's ball first-and-10 on B42. The defensive team takes possession at the spot of the kick.

A.R. 11.10 Fourth-and-10 on B35. A field-goal attempt is kicked from the B42, and is missed and:

a) the ball rolls dead on the B10.
   Ruling: B's ball first-and-10 on B42.

b) B1 touches and downs the ball on the B10.
   Ruling: B's ball first-and-10 on B10.

c) B1 fair catches the ball on the B10.
   Ruling: B's ball first-and-10 on B10.

A.R. 11.11 Fourth-and-10 on B35. On a field-goal attempt B1 catches the ball on the B10 and:

a) returns the ball to the B24.
   Ruling: B's ball first-and-10 on B24. If the receiving team runs a missed field goal, it continues as any other play.

b) returns the ball to the 50.
   Ruling: B's ball first-and-10 on 50.

A.R. 11.12 Fourth-and-10 on B30. A field-goal attempt is kicked from the B37 and is partially blocked behind the line and the ball rolls out of bounds on the B5:

a) without touching any receiver beyond the line of scrimmage.
   Ruling: B's ball first-and-10 on the B37.

b) after touching a receiver beyond the line of scrimmage.
   Ruling: B's ball first-and-10 on the B5 (the spot of out of bounds).

A.R. 11.13 Fourth-and-10 on B21. A missed field goal is kicked from the B28 and hits in the end zone and bounces back into the field of play to the B3 where:

a) no receiver touches the ball.
   Ruling: Ball dead. B's ball first-and-10 on the B28.

b) receiver B1 falls on the ball at the B3.
   Ruling: Ball dead. B's ball first-and-10 on the B28.

c) B1 picks up the ball on the B3 and runs to the B10.
   Ruling: Ball dead. B's ball first-and-10 on the B28.

d) B1 picks up the ball, runs to the B10, is tackled and fumbles. A1 recovers and is downed on the B8.
Ruling: Ball dead. B's ball first-and-10 on the B28.

A.R. 11.14 Fourth-and-10 on B35. On a missed field-goal attempt B1 touches the ball on the B4 and the ball then rolls into the end zone (or over the end line) where it is declared dead in possession of Team B.
Ruling: Touchback. B's ball first-and-10 on B20.

A.R. 11.15 Fourth-and-two on B10. A field goal is good. B1 punched A2 on the scrimmage line.
Ruling: Option for Team A. Score for field goal or A's ball first-and-goal on B5. See 14-6. Disqualify B1. If a score taken, it is 15-yard penalty against Team B on kickoff (14-1-14).

Article 3   **Fair-Catch Kick.** The rules for a field-goal attempt from scrimmage apply to a field-goal attempt following a Fair Catch (a Fair-Catch Kick).

Exceptions:

(a) The fair-catch kick line for the kicking team is the yard line through the most forward point from which the ball is kicked.

(b) The fair-catch kick line for the receiving team is the yard line 10 yards in advance of the kicking team's fair-catch kick line.

Note: A fair-catch kick is not a free kick. The kicking team cannot get the ball unless it has first been touched or possessed by the receivers.

A.R. 11.16 On a fair-catch kick from the B45, kicker A1 touches and falls on the ball on the B33 without any receiver touching the ball.
Ruling: B's ball first-and-10 on the B45 (the previous spot). The clock is started when the ball is kicked.

A.R. 11.17 On a fair-catch kick from the B45, the ball goes out of bounds on the B10:

a) without touching any player.
    Ruling: B's ball first-and-10 on the B45. The clock starts when the ball is kicked.

b) after touching any kicking team player.
    Ruling: B's ball first-and-10 on the B45. The clock starts when the ball is kicked.

Article 4   **No Tee.** An artificial or manufactured tee shall not be permitted to assist in the execution of a field goal.

Article 5   **Ball Next in Play.** After a field goal, the team scored upon will receive the kickoff. See 6-1-1-a.

Section 5   **SAFETY**

Article 1   **Safety.** It is a Safety:

(a) if the offense commits a foul in its own end zone; or

(b) when an impetus by a team sends the ball behind its own goal line, and the ball is dead in the end zone in its possession or the ball is out of bounds behind the goal line.

Exceptions:

It is not a safety:

(1) If a forward pass from behind the line of scrimmage is incomplete in the end zone.

(2) If a defensive player, in the field of play, intercepts a pass or catches or recovers a fumble, backward pass, scrimmage kick, free kick, or fair catch kick, and his original momentum carries him into his end zone where the ball is declared dead in his team's possession. The ball belongs to the defensive team at the spot where the ball was intercepted, caught, or recovered.

(a) If a player of the team which intercepts, catches, or recovers the ball commits a foul in the end zone, it is a safety.

(b) If a player who intercepts, catches, or recovers the ball throws a completed illegal forward pass from the end zone, the ball remains alive. If his opponent intercepts the illegal pass thrown from the end zone, the ball remains alive. If he scores, it is a touchdown.

(c) If a player of the team which intercepts, catches, or recovers the ball commits a foul in the field of play, and the ball becomes dead in the end zone, the basic spot is the spot of the change of possession. See A.R. 11.16.

(d) If the spot where possession changed is inside the one-yard line, the ball is to be spotted at the one-yard line.

■ **Supplemental Note**

The impetus is always attributed to the offense, unless the defense creates a new force that sends the ball behind its own goal line by muffing a ball which is at rest or nearly at rest, or by illegally batting or illegally kicking a ball (3-15-3).

A.R. 11.18 Second-and-10 on A6. Quarterback A1 throws a backward pass which is batted by defensive B1. The ball goes out of bounds behind the goal line.
Ruling: Safety. Legal bat and no change of impetus.

A.R. 11.19 Defensive B1 muffs a punt on his 7-yard line. In attempting to recover he forces the ball (new impetus) into his end zone. See 3-14-3.

a) where he recovers and is downed there.
   Ruling: Safety.

b) where he recovers and advances.
   Ruling: Legal advance.

c) where kicking team player recovers.
   Ruling: Touchdown.

A.R. 11.20 Defensive B1 catches a punt on the B4. He fumbles the ball on the B4 and kicking team player A1 bats the loose ball. The ball rolls over the end line.
Ruling: Touchback. See 11-6-1 and 12-1-6.

A.R. 11.21 Defensive B1 fumbles after catching a punt on the B5 and it crosses his goal line. Kicking team player A1 recovers while he is touching the sideline.
Ruling: Safety. If it had been a muff (no new impetus or change of possession) and the same situation, it would be a touchback (11-6-1).

A.R. 11.22 Second-and-10 on B20. Defensive B1 intercepts a legal forward pass on the B2. His momentum carries him into the end zone where he is downed.
Ruling: B's ball first-and-10 on B2.

A.R. 11.23 Second-and-10 on B20. Defensive B1 intercepts a legal forward pass on the B4 and his intercepting momentum carries him into the end zone. He then runs it out to the B35.
Ruling: B's ball first-and-10 on B35.

A.R. 11.24 Second-and-10 on B20. Defensive B1 intercepts a pass on the B6 and his momentum carries him into the end zone where he is tackled, fumbles and passing team player A1 recovers there.
Ruling: Touchdown Team A. Kickoff on A30.

A.R. 11.25 Second-and-10 on B20. Defensive B1 intercepts a legal forward pass on the B4 and his momentum carries him into the end zone where he is downed.

a) B2 clipped in the end zone.
   Ruling: Safety.

b) B2 clipped on the B2.
   Ruling: B's ball first-and-10 on B1.

A.R. 11.26 Second-and-15 on A4. Runner A1 fumbles a handoff on his 5-yard line. The ball rolls into the end zone where A1 bats or kicks the ball across the end line to prevent a recovery by the defense.
Ruling: Safety, whether the penalty is enforced from the spot of the foul or is declined (11-2-1-S.N. 2).

A.R. 11.27 Receiver B1 recovers a free kick in his end zone. While advancing, he fumbles while still in the end zone. The fumble is on the ground on the B2 where B3 deliberately kicks it.
Ruling: Safety (8-4-4). The spot of enforcement is from the spot of the fumble.

A.R. 11.28 B1 catches a kickoff and makes a forward pass from behind his goal line.
Ruling: Safety. Team A may intercept and advance.

A.R. 11.29 Second-and-15 on A2. Runner A1 is downed two yards behind his goal line.

a) A2 holds anywhere in the field.
   Ruling: Safety (14-1-11).

b) B1 holds at A1.
   Ruling: A's ball first-and-10 on A6 (12-1-4-Pen. and 14-1-12-Exc. 7).

A.R. 11.30 Second-and-16 on A4. Quarterback A1 drops back to pass and throws a legal forward pass complete to end A2 who runs for a touchdown. Prior to the completion offensive tackle A3 holds in the end zone.
Ruling: No touchdown. Safety.

Article 2   **Ball in Play After Safety.** After a safety, the team scored upon must put the ball in play by a free kick (punt, dropkick, or placekick) from its 20-yard line. An artificial or manufactured tee cannot be used. See 6-1-2 and 6-1-3.

Exception: For extension of either half, see 4-8-2-j.

Section 6   **TOUCHBACK**

Note: A touchback, while not a score, is included in this rule because, like scoring plays, it is a case of a ball that is dead on or behind a goal line (3-15-2).

Article 1   **Definition.** It is a Touchback if the ball is dead on or behind the goal line a team is defending, provided that the impetus comes from an opponent, and that it is not a touchdown or an incomplete forward pass.

Article 2   **Touchback Situations.** When a team provides the impetus (3-15-3) that sends a loose ball behind its opponent's goal line, it is a touchback:

(a) if the ball is dead in the opponent's possession in its end zone; or

(b) if the ball is out of bounds behind the goal line (see 7-5-6-c); or

(c) if a scrimmage kick has not been touched by a player of the receiving team beyond the line of scrimmage, and the ball (i) touches the ground on or behind the receiver's goal line, (ii) touches a player of the kicking team who is touching the ground on or behind the receiver's goal line, or (iii) touches a player of the kicking team who has touched the ground on or behind the receiver's goal line and has not re-established himself in the field of play (see 11-4-2-b for exception for a missed field goal from beyond the 20-yard line); or

(d) if any legal or illegal kick touches the receivers' goal posts, crossbar, or uprights, other than one which scores a field goal; or

(e) if the kickers interfere with the opportunity to catch an airborne kick or with a fair catch behind the receivers' goal line (10-1-1 and 10-2-4-Note); or

(f) if a player of the kicking team illegally catches or recovers a scrimmage kick in the field of play, and carries the ball across the goal line, or touches the goal line with any part of his body while in possession of the ball. For exception for a missed field goal from beyond the 20-yard line, see 11-4-2-b.

Note 1: If the impetus is a scrimmage kick, and there has been a spot of first touching by the kickers beyond the receivers' 20-yard line, the receivers shall have the option of taking possession of the ball at the spot of first touching.

Note 2: The impetus is not from a kick if a muff, bat, juggle, or illegal kick of any kicked ball (by a player of either team) creates a new momentum which sends it on, above, or behind the goal line. See 3-15-3-Note.

A.R. 11.31 Quarterback A1 throws a legal pass which is intercepted in the end zone by defensive B1. B1 tries to run it out and is downed in the end zone.
Ruling: Touchback. B's ball first-and-10 on B20.

A.R. 11.32 A punt is caught in end zone by defensive B1 who tries to run it out. He is tackled, fumbles and kicking team player A1 recovers in end zone.
Ruling: Touchdown for A1.

A.R. 11.33 Fourth-and-10 on B35. A1 is touching the goal line with his foot when he downs the punted ball on the 1-yard line in the field of play.
Ruling: Touchback.

Article 3   **Ball Next in Play.** After a touchback, the team that has been awarded a touchback next snaps the ball at its 20-yard line from any point on or between the inbounds lines.

Player
Conduct

Rule 12

Player Conduct

Section 1 **BLOCKING, USE OF HANDS, ARMS, AND BODY**

Article 1 A player of either team may block (obstruct or impede) an opponent at any time, provided that the act is not:

(a) pass interference

(b) illegal contact

(c) fair catch interference

(d) clipping against a non-runner

(e) an illegal chop block

(f) an illegal crackback block

(g) an illegal low block during a free kick, scrimmage kick, or after a change of possession

(h) unnecessary roughness

(i) roughing the passer

(j) an illegal cut block

(k) roughing the kicker

(l) offensive or defensive holding

(m) illegal use of hands

(n) tripping

(o) illegal peel back block

(p) illegal blindside block

A.R. 12.1 Defensive B1 blocks offensive A1 which allows B2 to recover a loose ball.
Ruling: Legal block. Cannot use hands unless it is a personal attempt to recover, but may block (12-1-5).

Article 2 An offensive player cannot obstruct or impede an opponent by grasping him with his hands or encircling any part of a defender's body with his arms, except in the following situations:

(a) If he is a runner. A runner may ward off opponents with his hands and arms. He also may lay his hand on a teammate or push him into an opponent, but he may not grasp or hold on to a teammate; or

(b) During a loose ball that has touched the ground. An offensive player may use his hands/arms legally to block or otherwise push or pull an opponent out of the way in a **personal** attempt to recover the ball. See specific fumble, pass, or kick rules and especially 6-2-1; or

(c) During a kick. A kicking team player may use his hands/arms to ward off or to push or pull aside a receiver who is legally or illegally attempting to obstruct his attempt to proceed downfield; or

(d) During a legal block.

Penalty: For illegal use of hands, arms, or body by the offense: Loss of 10 yards.

Article 3   An offensive player is permitted to block an opponent by contacting him with his head, shoulders, hands, and/or outer surface of the forearm, or with any other part of his body.

A blocker may use his arms, or open or closed hands, to contact an opponent on or outside the opponent's frame (the body of an opponent below the neck that is presented to the blocker). If a blocker's arms or hands are outside an opponent's frame, it is a foul if the blocker materially restricts him. The blocker immediately must work to bring his hands inside the opponent's frame, and as the play develops, the blocker is permitted to work for and maintain his position against an opponent, provided that he does not illegally clip or illegally push from behind.

Article 4   An offensive blocker cannot:

(a) thrust his hands forward above the frame of an opponent to contact him on the neck, face, or head (Note: Contact in close-line play that is not prolonged and sustained is not a foul unless the opponent's head is pinned back by direct and forcible contact);

(b) charge or fall into the back of an opponent above the waist, or use his hands or arms to push an opponent from behind in a manner that affects his movement, except in close-line play (the guideline for officials to use for illegal use of hands in the back above the waist is: if either hand is on the back, it is a foul. If both hands are on the opponent's side, it is not a foul);

Note: The prohibition applies to a player of the kicking team while the ball is in flight during a scrimmage kick.

(c) use his hands or arms to materially restrict an opponent or alter the defender's path or angle of pursuit. Material restrictions include but are not limited to:
   (i)   grabbing or tackling an opponent;
   (ii) hooking, jerking, twisting, or turning him; or
   (iii) pulling him to the ground.

Penalty: For holding, illegal use of hands, arms, or body by the offense: Loss of 10 yards.

Blocking notes:

1. When a defensive player is held by an offensive player during the following situations, offensive holding will not be called:
   (a) if the runner is being tackled simultaneously by another defensive player;
   (b) if the runner simultaneously goes out of bounds;
   (c) if a fair catch is made simultaneously;
   (d) if the action clearly occurs after a forward pass has been thrown to a receiver beyond the line of scrimmage;
   (e) if the action occurs away from the point of attack and not within close-line play;

(f) if a free kick results in a touchback;

(g) if a scrimmage kick simultaneously becomes a touchback;

(h) if the action is part of a double-team block in close-line play.

Exception: Holding will be called if the opponent is pulled to the ground by one or both of the blockers.

(i) if, during a defensive charge, a defensive player uses a "rip" technique that puts an offensive player in a position that would normally be holding.

Exception: Holding will be called if the defender's feet are taken away from him by the offensive player's action.

2. If a blocker falls on or pushes down a defender whose momentum is carrying him to the ground, offensive holding will not be called unless the blocker prevents the defender from rising from the ground.

3. If the official has not seen the entire action that sends a defender to the ground, offensive holding will not be called.

Article 5   No offensive player may:

(a) lift a runner to his feet or pull him in any direction at any time; or

(b) use interlocking interference, by grasping a teammate or by using his hands or arms to encircle the body of a teammate; or

(c) trip an opponent; or

(d) push or throw his body against a teammate to aid him in an attempt to obstruct an opponent or to recover a loose ball

Penalty: For assisting the runner or for interlocking interference, <u>tripping, illegal use of hands, arms, or body by the offense</u>: Loss of 10 yards.

A.R. 12.2 Second and goal on B2. Runner A1 gets to the line of scrimmage and is stopped but A2, who is behind him, pushes him from behind and shoves him over the goal line.

Ruling: Touchdown.

Article 6   A defensive player may not:

(a) tackle or hold any opponent other than a runner. Otherwise, he may use his hands, arms, or body only to defend or protect himself against an obstructing opponent in an attempt to reach a runner. After a loose ball has touched the ground, a defensive player may legally block or otherwise use his hands or arms to push or pull an opponent out of the way in a personal attempt to recover the ball.

(b) on a punt, field-goal attempt, or Try-kick attempt, grab and pull an offensive player out of the way which allows another defensive player(s) (B2) to shoot the gap (pull and shoot) in an attempt to block the kick, unless the defensive player (B1) is advancing towards the kicker.

(c) thrust his hands forward above the frame of an opponent to contact him on the neck, face, or head (Note: Contact in close-line play that is not prolonged and sustained is not a foul, unless the opponent's head is pinned back by direct and forcible contact.

Exception 1: See Rule 8, Section 4, Articles 1-4 for legal and illegal contact against an eligible receiver.

Within the five-yard zone, a defender may not make original contact in the back of a receiver, nor may he use his hands or arms to hang on to or encircle a receiver. The defender cannot extend an arm(s) to cut off or hook a receiver causing contact that impedes and restricts the receiver as the play develops, nor may he maintain contact after the receiver has moved beyond a point that is even with the defender.

Beyond the five-yard zone, if the player who receives the snap remains in the pocket with the ball, a defender may use his hands or arms only to defend or protect himself against impending contact caused by a receiver. If the receiver attempts to evade the defender, the defender cannot chuck him, or extend an arm(s) to cut off or hook him, causing contact that redirects, restricts, or impedes the receiver in any way.

Beyond the five-yard zone, incidental contact may exist between receiver and defender as long as it does not materially affect or significantly impede the receiver, creating a distinct advantage.

Exception 2: See Rule 8, Section 4, Article 5 for legal and illegal cut blocks.

Note 1: Once the quarterback or receiver of the snap hands off, is tackled, throws a forward or backward pass, loses possession of the ball by a fumble or a muff that touches the ground, or if the quarterback leaves the pocket area (see 3-25), the restrictions on the defensive team relative to offensive receivers (illegal contact, illegal cut block) will end.

Note 2: Whenever a team presents an apparent punting formation, defensive action that would normally constitute illegal contact (chuck beyond five yards) will no longer be considered a foul.

Penalty: For illegal contact or holding by the defense: Loss of five yards and automatic first down.

Penalty: For illegal cut block by the defense: Loss of 15 yards and automatic first down. (Personal Foul)

■ **Supplemental Notes**

(1) An eligible pass receiver who takes a position more than two yards outside of his own tackle (flexed receiver) may not be blocked below the waist (illegal cut), unless the quarterback hands off, is tackled, pitches the ball to a back, or if the quarterback leaves the pocket area.

(2) The unnecessary use of the hands by the defense, except as provided in Article 4, is illegal and is commonly used in lieu of a legal block (Article 5) (See 12-2-2).

(3) Any offensive player who pretends to possess the ball and/or one to whom a teammate pretends to give the ball, may be tackled provided he is crossing his scrimmage line between the offensive tackles of a normal tight offensive line.

A.R. 12.3 Second-and-10 on B40. Defensive B1 holds offensive end A1 on the line of scrimmage. Quarterback A2 can't throw the ball and is tackled at the 50.
Ruling: Not a forward pass. Enforcement is from the previous spot. A's ball first-and-10 on B35.

A.R. 12.4 Second-and-10 on A40. Eligible end A1 goes downfield to the B45 and is contacted (chucked) by defender B1 as A1 attempts to evade him. The pass falls incomplete.
Ruling: A's ball first-and-10 on A45. Illegal contact. Eligible receiver A1 is not considered an obstructing player as he was more than five yards beyond line of scrimmage.

A.R. 12.5 Second-and-10 on A40. Eligible receiver A1 is chucked by B1 at the scrimmage line. B1 then chucks back A2 on the A44 prior to the pass. The pass then falls incomplete.

Ruling: Legal use of hands as A1 and A2 were not the same player.

A.R. 12.6 Second-and-10 on A30. Eligible pass receiver A1 takes a position three yards outside his own tackle and is blocked below the waist at line of scrimmage. The pass falls incomplete.

Ruling: Illegal cut as eligible receiver was more than two yards outside of his tackle. Fifteen-yard penalty. A's ball first-and-10 on A45.

A.R. 12.7 Second-and-10 on A30. Eligible pass receiver A1 lines up one yard outside of his own tackle and is blocked below the waist at the line of scrimmage. Pass falls incomplete.

Ruling: Legal block as receiver was lined up within two yards of the tackle. A's ball third-and-10 on A30.

A.R. 12.8 During a pass *behind* the line (forward or backward), B1 uses his hands on potential receiver A1 who is *behind* A's line. B1 is not using his hands to ward off A1, to push or pull A1 out of the way in order to get to the runner (passer), or to push or pull him out of the way in an actual attempt to catch or recover a loose ball.

Ruling: Illegal use of hands by the defense. Loss of five yards and first down for Team A (14-8-5).

Article 7   No defensive player may trip an opponent.

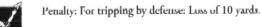

Penalty: For tripping by defense: Loss of 10 yards.

Article 8   A player may not bat or punch:

(a) a loose ball (in field of play) toward opponent's goal line;

(b) a loose ball (that has touched the ground) in any direction, if it is in either end zone;

(c) a backward pass in flight may not be batted forward by an offensive player.

Exception: A forward pass in flight may be tipped, batted, or deflected in any direction by any eligible player at any time.

Note: If a forward pass that is controlled by an airborne player prior to completing the catch is thrown forward, it is an illegal bat. If it is caught by a teammate or intercepted by an opponent, the ball remains alive. If it is not caught, the ball is dead when it hits the ground.

Penalty: For illegal batting or punching the ball: Loss of 10 yards. For enforcement, treat as a foul during a backward pass or fumble (see 8-7).

Article 9   No player may deliberately kick any loose ball or ball in player's possession.

Penalty: For illegally kicking the ball: Loss of 10 yards. For enforcement, treat as a foul during a backward pass or fumble (see 8-7).

■ Supplemental Notes

(1) If a loose ball is touched by any part of a player's leg (including knee), it is not considered kicking and is treated merely as touching.

(2) If the penalty for an illegal bat or kick is declined, the procedure is the same as though the ball had been merely muffed. However, if the act (impetus) sends the ball in touch, 3-15-3 applies.

(3) The penalty for Article 8 and 9, does not preclude a penalty for a palpably unfair act, when a deliberate kick or illegal bat actually prevents an opponent from recovering. See Palpably Unfair Act 12-3-3.

(4) The ball is not dead when an illegal kick is recovered.

A.R. 12.9 Second-and-15 on A2. Quarterback A1 fumbles a snap in the end zone. While the ball is loose on the ground there, A1 deliberately kicks it. The ball is last touched by B1 before going out of bounds on A's 2-yard line.
Ruling: Safety. See 7-5-6-d; 11-5-1; and 12-1-9.

Section 2   **PERSONAL FOULS**

Article 1   All players are prohibited from:

(a) striking with the fists;

(b) kicking or kneeing; or

(c) striking, swinging, or clubbing to the head, neck, or face with the heel, back, or side of the hand, wrist, arm, elbow, or clasped hands. See 12-2-3.

(d) grabbing the inside collar of the back of the shoulder pads or jersey, or the inside collar of the side of the shoulder pads or jersey, and immediately pulling down the runner. This does not apply to a runner who is in the tackle box or to a quarterback who is in the pocket.

Penalty: For fouls in a, b, c, and d: Loss of 15 yards. If any of the above acts is judged by the official(s) to be flagrant, the offender may be disqualified as long as the entire action is observed by the official(s).

Article 2   A defensive player shall not contact an opponent above the shoulders with the palm of his hands except to ward him off on the line. The exception applies only if it is not a repeated act against the same opponent during any one contact.

Article 3   A defensive player may use the palm of his hands on an opponent's head, neck, or face only to ward off or push him in an actual attempt to get at a loose ball.

Article 4 A player in blocking shall not strike an opponent below the shoulders with his forearm or elbows by turning the trunk of his body at the waist, pivoting or in any other way that is clearly unnecessary.

Penalty: For illegal use of the palm of the hands or for striking an opponent below the shoulders with the forearm or elbow: Loss of 15 yards.

Note: Any impermissible use of elbows, forearms, or knees shall be penalized under the unnecessary roughness rule; flagrantly unnecessary roughness shall be penalized under the same rule and the player disqualified.

A.R. 12.10 Second-and-10 on A30. Defensive player B1, on his initial charge, head slaps an offensive tackle on the helmet once with his open hand trying to get at runner A1. A1 is downed on the A35
Ruling: Illegal. A's ball first-and-10 on the 50.

A.R. 12.11 Second-and-10 on A30. Defensive player B1, on his initial charge, head slaps an offensive tackle on his helmet repeatedly with his open hand in trying to get at a runner. The runner is downed on the A35.
Ruling: Illegal. Loss of 15 yards. A's ball first-and-10 on the 50.

Article 5 No player shall twist, turn, or pull the facemask of an opponent in any direction.

Penalty: For twisting, turning, or pulling the mask: Loss of 15 yards. A personal foul. The player may be disqualified if the action is judged by the official(s) to be of a flagrant nature.

A.R. 12.12 Third-and-10 on A30. Runner A1 runs to the A33, where he is tackled by B1, who incidentally grasps A1's face mask on the tackle, but it is not a twist, turn, or pull.
Ruling: A's ball, fourth-and-seven, on A33. No Foul.

Article 6   No defensive player may run into or rough a kicker who kicks
             from behind his line unless such contact:

(a) is incidental to and after he has touched the kick in
    flight;

(b) is caused by the kicker's own motions;

(c) occurs during a quick kick;

(d) occurs during a kick or after a run behind the line;

(e) occurs after the kicker recovers a loose ball on the
    ground; or

(f) is caused because a defender is blocked into the
    kicker.

Penalty: For running into the kicker: Loss of five yards from
the previous spot, no automatic first down. (This is not a
personal foul). For roughing the kicker or holder, loss of 15
yards from the previous spot. (This is a personal foul, and
also disqualification if flagrant).

■ Supplemental Notes

(1) Avoiding the kicker is a primary responsibility of
    defensive players if they do not touch the kick.

(2) Any contact with the kicker by a single defensive
    player who has not touched the kick is running into
    the kicker.

(3) Any unnecessary roughness committed by defensive
    players is roughing the kicker. Severity of contact
    and potential for injury are to be considered.

(4) When two defensive players are making a bona fide
    attempt to block a kick from scrimmage (punt, drop
    kick, and/or placekick) and one of them runs into
    the kicker after the kick has left the kicker's foot at
    the same instant the second player blocks the kick,

the foul for running into the kicker shall *not* be enforced, unless in the judgment of the Referee, the player running into the kicker was clearly the direct cause of the kick being blocked.

(5) If in the judgment of the Referee any of the above action is unnecessary roughness, the penalty for roughing the kicker *shall* be enforced from the previous spot as a foul during a kick.

A.R. 12.13 Kicker A1 in punt formation muffs a snap. He recovers on the ground and then kicks. A1 is run into, blocked, or tackled by B1 who had started his action when A1 first recovered.
Ruling: Legal action by B1.

A.R. 12.14 A1 receives a snap. He starts to run but after a few strides, he kicks from behind his line. As A1 kicks, he is tackled or run into.
Ruling: The kicker is to be protected, but the Referee should use his judgment when ordinary line play carries an opponent into such a kicker or at any time when it is not obvious that a kick is to be made (quick kick).

A.R. 12.15 Fourth-and-12 on B30. On a field-goal attempt which is not good, receiver B1 runs into the kicker without touching the ball.
Ruling: A's ball fourth-and-7 on B25. Running into the kicker. If the field goal had been good, no penalty would be enforced on the succeeding kickoff, since it was not a personal foul.

| Article 7 | No player shall fall upon any prostrate player (other than the runner) or upon runner after the ball is dead.. |

Penalty: For piling on: Loss of 15 yards.

Note: An official should prevent piling on a prostrate or helpless runner before the ball is dead. When opponents in close proximity to such a runner are about to pile on, and further advance is improbable, the official covering should sound his whistle for a dead ball, in order to prevent further play and roughness. See 7-4-1-d.

A.R. 12.16 The holder of a Try-kick is run into or piled on and the act is not incidental to blocking the kick.
Ruling: Unnecessary roughness. Such a player is obviously out of play unless the kick is blocked, and even then until he arises and participates in play. See 14-1-14 and 14-6-Exc. 6.

Article 8   There shall be no unnecessary roughness. This shall include, but will not be limited to:

    (a) striking an opponent anywhere above the knee with the foot or any part of the leg below the knee with a whipping motion;

    (b) <u>contacting a running</u> out of bounds;

    <u>Note: Defensive players must make an effort to avoid contact. Players on defense are responsible for knowing when a runner has crossed the boundary line, except in doubtful cases where he might step on a boundary line and continue parallel with it.</u>

    (c) a member of the receiving team cannot go out of bounds and contact a kicking team player out of bounds. If this occurs on a kick from scrimmage, post-possession rules would apply if appropriate (9-5-1);

    (d) running or diving into, or throwing the body against or on a ball carrier who falls or slips to the ground untouched and makes no attempt to advance, before or after the ball is dead;

    (e) unnecessarily running, diving into, cutting, or throwing the body against or on a player who (i) is out of the play or (ii) should not have reasonably anticipated such contact by an opponent, before or after the ball is dead; or throwing the runner to the ground after the ball is dead;

(f) If a player uses any part of his helmet (including the top/crown and forehead/"hairline" parts) or face-mask to butt, spear, or ram an opponent violently or unnecessarily. Although such violent or unnecessary use of the helmet and facemask is impermissible against any opponent, game officials will give special attention in administering this rule to protecting those players who are in virtually defenseless postures, including but not limited to:

(1) Forcibly hitting the defenseless player's head, neck, or face with the helmet or facemask, regardless of whether the defensive player also uses his arms to tackle the defenseless player by encircling or grasping him; or

(2) Lowering the head and violently or unnecessarily making forcible contact with the "hairline" or forehead part of the helmet against any part of the defenseless player's body; or

(3) "Launching" (springing forward and upward) into a defenseless player, or otherwise striking him in a way that causes the defensive player's helmet or facemask to forcibly strike the defenseless player's head, neck, or face—even if the initial contact of the defender's helmet or facemask is lower than the defenseless player's neck. (Examples: a defender buries his facemask into a defenseless player's high chest area, but the defender's trajectory as he leaps into the defenseless player causes the defender's helmet to strike the defenseless player violently in the head or face; or a defender, using a face-on posture or with his head slightly lowered, hits a defenseless player in an area below the defenseless player's neck, then the defender's head moves upward, resulting in strong contact by the defender's mask

or helmet with the defenseless player's head,
neck, or face [an example is the so-called "dip
and rip" technique]).

*Note: The provisions of section (f) do not prohibit inciden-
tal contact by the mask or non-crown parts of the helmet in
the course of a conventional tackle on an opponent.*

(g) if the initial force of the contact by a defender's
helmet (including facemask), forearm, or shoulder is
to the head or neck area of a defenseless player.

*Note: Defenseless players in (f) and (g) shall include (i) a
player in the act of or just after throwing a pass; (ii) a
receiver catching or attempting to catch a pass; (iii) a
runner already in the grasp of a tackler and whose forward
progress has been stopped; (iv) a kickoff or punt returner
attempting to field a kick in the air; and (v) a player on the
ground at the end of a play.*

(h) If a receiver has completed a catch and has not had
time to protect himself, a defensive player is prohibited from launching (springing forward and upward)
into him in a way that causes the defensive player's
helmet, facemask, shoulder, or forearm to forcibly
strike the receiver's head or neck area—even if the
initial contact of the defender's helmet, facemask,
shoulder, or forearm is lower than the receiver's neck.

*Note: Launching is defined as springing forward and
upward by a player who leaves his feet to make contact on
the receiver.*

(i) a kicker/punter, who is standing still or fading backwards after the ball has been kicked, is out of the
play and must not be unnecessarily contacted by the
receiving team through the end of the play or until
he assumes a distinctly defensive position. During
the kick or during the return, if the initial force of

the contact by a defender's helmet (including face-mask), forearm, or shoulder is to the head or neck area of the kicker/punter, it is a foul.

(j) any player who <u>grabs a helmet opening</u> of an opponent and forcibly twists, <u>turns, or pulls</u> his head.

(k) Illegal contact with the helmet against the knee of the snapper during an attempt for a field goal or kick try.

Penalty: For unnecessary roughness: Loss of 15 yards. The player may be disqualified if the action is judged by the official(s) to be flagrant.

Note: If in doubt about a roughness call or potentially dangerous tactics, the covering official(s) should always call unnecessary roughness.

A.R. 12.17 Third-and-20 on A30. Runner A1 runs to the A33, where he is tackled by B1, who hooks his fingers under the front of the runner's helmet, but not his facemask, and forcibly twists his head.
Ruling: 15 yards for unnecessary roughness. It is an automatic first down. A's ball first-and-10 on A48.

Article 9
There shall be no clipping from behind below the waist against a non-runner. This does not apply to offensive blocking in close-line play where it is legal to clip above the knee(s), but it is illegal to clip at or below the knee(s).

Penalty: For clipping: Loss of 15 yards.

■ **Supplemental Notes**

(1) Close-line play is that which occurs in an area extending laterally to the position originally occupied by the offensive tackles and longitudinally three yards on either side of each line of scrimmage.

(2) In close-line play, if an offensive player's block (legal or illegal) is followed by the blocker rolling up on the

back of the leg(s) of the defender, the action is illegal and is considered unnecessary roughness.

Exception: An offensive lineman may not clip a defender who, at the snap, is aligned on the line of scrimmage opposite another offensive lineman who is more than one position away when the defender is responding to the flow of the ball away from the blocker.

Example: Tackle cannot clip nose tackle on sweep away.

(3) Doubtful cases involving a side block or the opponent turning his back as the block is being made are to be judged according to whether the opponent was able to see or ward off the blocker.

(4) The use of hands from behind above the waist on a non-runner is illegal use of hands (see 12-1-3).

(5) The use of hands on the back is not a foul when it is by:
   a) one of the kickers in warding off a receiver, while going downfield under a kick, or
   b) any player in an actual personal legal attempt to recover a loose ball.

(6) It is not considered clipping if:
   a) a blocker is moving in the same direction as an opponent, and has initial contact on the side of the opponent and then continues to contact with the opponent below his waist from behind with any part of his body, or
   b) in any case if an official has not observed the blocker's initial contact.

A.R. 12.18 Second-and-10 on B30 B1 is hit from behind, below the waist, at the B25 by A2 throwing his body across the back of B1's legs. Runner A1 is downed on B15.
Ruling: Clipping. A's ball second-and-20 on B40.

A.R. 12.19 Second-and-10 on B30. A2 pushes B1 from behind above the waist at the B25. Runner A1 is down on B15. **Ruling:** Illegal <u>block above the waist</u>, A's ball second-and-15 on B35.

Article 10 At the snap, an offensive player who is aligned in a position more than two yards laterally outside an offensive tackle, or a player who is in a backfield position at the snap and then moves to a position more than two yards laterally outside a tackle, may not clip an opponent anywhere, nor may he contact an opponent below the waist if the blocker is moving toward the position where the ball was snapped from, and the contact occurs within an area five yards on either side of the line of scrimmage.

Note 1: A player aligned more than two yards laterally outside a tackle at the snap is designated as being flexed.

Note 2: If runner (passer) scrambles on the play, significantly changing the original direction (broken play), the crackback block is legal.

Penalty: Illegal crackback block: Loss of 15 yards.

A.R. 12.20 Second-and-10 on A40. Flanker A1 sets up five yards outside of offensive tackle A2. At snap A1 comes back and crackback blocks B1. Contact is made at the A38 behind the offensive tackle's original position. Runner goes to 50. **Ruling:** A's ball second-and-25 on A25. Illegal crackback block. Penalize from previous spot.

Article 11 When a player who is aligned in the tackle box at the snap moves to a position outside the box, he cannot initiate contact on the side and below the waist on an opponent if:

a) the blocker is moving toward his own end line; and

b) he approaches the opponent from behind or from the side.

Note: If the near shoulder of the blocker contacts the front of his opponent's body, the "peel back" block is legal.

Penalty: For illegal "peel back" block: Loss of 15 yards.

Article 12   It is an illegal "blindside" block if the initial force of the contact by a blocker's helmet, forearm, or shoulder is to the head or neck area of an opponent when:

(a) the blocker is moving toward his own endline; and

(b) he approaches the opponent from behind or from the side.

Penalty: For illegal "blindside" block: Loss of 15 yards.

Article 13   Because the act of passing often puts the quarterback (or any other player attempting a pass) in a position where he is particularly vulnerable to injury, special rules against roughing the passer apply. The Referee has principal responsibility for enforcing these rules. Any physical acts against passers during or just after a pass which, in the Referee's judgment, are unwarranted by the circumstances of the play will be called as fouls. The Referee will be guided by the following principles:

(1) Roughing will be called if, in the Referee's judgment, a pass rusher clearly should have known that the ball had already left the passer's hand before contact was made; pass rushers are responsible for being aware of the position of the ball in passing situations; the Referee will use the release of the ball from the passer's hand as his guideline that the passer is now fully protected; once a pass has been released by a passer, a rushing defender may make direct contact with the passer only up through the rusher's first step after such release (prior to second step hitting the ground); thereafter the rusher must be making an attempt to avoid contact and must not continue to "drive through" or otherwise forcibly contact the passer; incidental or inadvertent contact by a player who is easing up or being blocked into the passer will not be considered significant.

(2) A rushing defender is prohibited from committing such intimidating and punishing acts as "stuffing" a passer into the ground or unnecessarily wrestling or driving him down after the passer has thrown the ball, even if the rusher makes his initial contact with the passer within the one-step limitation provided for in (1) above. When tackling a passer who is in a virtually defenseless posture (e.g., during or just after throwing a pass), a defensive player must not unnecessarily or violently throw him down and land on top of him with all or most of the defender's weight. Instead, the defensive player must strive to wrap up or cradle the passer with the defensive player's arms.

(3) In covering the passer position, Referees will be particularly alert to fouls in which defenders impermissibly use the helmet and/or facemask to hit the passer, or use hands, arms, or other parts of the body to hit the passer in the head, neck, or face (see also the other unnecessary-roughness rules covering these subjects). A defensive player must not use his facemask or other part of his helmet against a passer who is in a virtually defenseless posture—for example, (a) forcibly hitting the passer's head, neck, or face with the helmet or facemask, regardless of whether the defensive player also uses his arms to tackle the passer by encircling or grasping him, or (b) lowering the head and violently or unnecessarily making forcible contact with the "hairline" or forehead part of the helmet against any part of the passer's body. This rule does not prohibit incidental contact by the mask or non-crown parts of the helmet in the course of a conventional tackle on a passer. A defensive player must not "launch" himself (spring forward and upward) into a passer, or otherwise strike him in a way that causes the defensive player's helmet or facemask to forcibly strike the

passer's head, neck, or face—even if the initial contact of the defender's helmet or facemask is lower than the passer's neck. Examples: (a) a defender buries his facemask into a passer's high chest area, but the defender's trajectory as he leaps into the passer causes the defender's helmet to strike the passer violently in the head or face; (b) a defender, using a face-on posture or with head slightly lowered, hits a passer in an area below the passer's neck, then the defender's head moves upward, resulting in strong contact by the defender's mask or helmet with the passer's head, neck, or face (one example of this is the so-called "dip-and-rip" technique).

(4) A defensive player is prohibited from clubbing the arm of a passer during a pass or just after a pass has been thrown; however, a defensive player may grasp, pull, or otherwise make normal contact with a passer's arm in attempting to tackle him;

(5) A rushing defender is prohibited from forcibly hitting in the knee area or below a passer who has one or both feet on the ground, even if the initial contact is above the knee. It is not a foul if the defender is blocked (or fouled) into the passer and has no opportunity to avoid him;

Note 1: A defender cannot initate a roll or lunge and forcibly hit the passer in the knee area or below, even if he is being contacted by another player.

Note 2: It is not a foul if the defender swipes, wraps, or grabs a passer in the knee area or below in an attempt to tackle him.

(6) The Referee must blow the play dead as soon as the passer is clearly in the grasp and control of any tackler behind the line, and the passer's safety is in jeopardy;

(7) A passer who is standing still or fading backwards after the ball has left his hand is obviously out of the play and must not be unnecessarily contacted by the defense through the end of the play or until the passer becomes a blocker, or until he becomes a runner upon taking a lateral from a teammate or picking up a loose ball, or, in the event of a change of possession on the play, until the passer assumes a distinctly defensive position. <u>At any time after the change of possession, if the initial force of the contact by a defender's helmet (including facemask), forearm, or shoulder is to the head or neck area of the quarterback it is a foul.</u>

(8) When the passer goes outside the pocket area and either continues moving with the ball (without attempting to advance the ball as a runner) or throws while on the run, he loses the protection of the one-step rule provided for in (1 and 5) above, but he remains covered by all the other special protections afforded to a passer in the pocket (numbers 2, 3, 4, 6, and 7), as well as the regular unnecessary-roughness rules applicable to all player positions. If the passer stops behind the line and clearly establishes a passing posture, he will then be covered by all of the special protections for passers.

Penalty: For Roughing the Passer: Loss of 15 yards from the previous spot; disqualification if flagrant.

Note 1: If in doubt about a roughness call or potentially dangerous tactic on the quarterback, the Referee should always call roughing the passer.

Note 2: See 8-6-2 for personal fouls prior to completion or interception.

A.R. 12.21 Passer A1 is run into or tackled by defensive B1 after a pass. B1 had started his action prior to pass.

Ruling: A legal action, unless the official rules that B1 had a reasonable chance to avoid or minimize the contact and made no attempt to do so.

Article 14   Blocks below the waist are prohibited in the following situations:

(a) By players of either team after a change of possession; or

(b) By players of the kicking team after a Free Kick, Safety Kick, Fair-Catch Kick, Punt, Field-Goal Attempt, or Try Kick; or

(c) By players of the receiving team during a down in which there is a Free Kick, Safety Kick, Fair-Catch Kick, Punt, Field-Goal Attempt, or Try Kick.

Exception: Immediately at the snap, players on the receiving team who are on the line of scrimmage and lined up on or inside the normal tight end position are permitted to block low during a Punt, Field-Goal Attempt, or Try Kick.

Note: Illegal contact with the helmet against the knee of the snapper during a Field-Goal Attempt or a Try Kick is unnecessary roughness (see 12-2-8-j).

Penalty: For illegally blocking below the waist: Loss of 15 yards.

A.R. 12.22 Third-and-6 on B26. B1 intercepts a forward pass in the end zone and runs it out to the B31. During B1's run, A2 blocks B3 low from the side at B28, so that A4 could tackle B1 at the B31.

Ruling: Illegal block. B's ball first-and-10 on B46 (12-2-13).

Article 15   A player may not use a helmet (that is no longer worn by anyone) as a weapon to strike, swing at, or throw at an opponent.

Penalty: For illegal use of helmet as a weapon: Loss of 15 yards and automatic disqualification.

Article 16 A chop block is a foul by the offense in which one offense player (designated as A1 for purposes of this rule) blocks a defensive player in the area of the thigh or lower while another offensive player (A2) occupies that same defensive player in one of the circumstances described in subsections (1) through (10) below.

(1) On a forward pass play, A1 chops a defensive player while the defensive player is physically engaged <u>above the waist</u> by the blocking attempt of A2.

(2) On a forward pass play in which A2 physically engages a defensive player <u>above the waist</u> with a blocking attempt, A1 chops the defensive player after the contact by A2 has been broken and while A2 is still confronting the defensive player.

(3) On a forward pass play, A1 chops a defensive player while A2 confronts the defensive player in a pass-blocking posture but is not physically engaged with the defensive player (a "lure").

(4) On a forward pass play, A1 blocks a defensive player in the area of the thigh or lower, and A2, simultaneously or immediately after the block by A1, engages the defensive player high.

Note: Each of the above circumstances in subsections (1) through (4), which describes a chop-block foul on a forward-pass play, also applies on a play in which an offensive player indicates an apparent attempt to pass block but the play ultimately becomes a run.

(5) On a running play, A1 is lined up in the backfield at the snap and subsequently chops a defensive player engaged above the waist by A2, and such block occurs on or behind the line of scrimmage in an area extending laterally to the positions originally occupied by the tight end on either side.

(6) On a running play, A1, an offensive lineman, chops a

defensive player after the defensive player has been engaged by A2 (high or low), and the initial alignment of A2 is more than one position away from A1. This rule applies only when the block occurs at a time when the flow of the play is clearly away from A1.

(7) On a kicking play, A1 chops a defensive player while the defensive player is physically engaged <u>above the waist</u> by the blocking attempt of A2.

(8) On a kicking play in which A2 physically engages a defensive player <u>above the waist</u> with a blocking attempt, A1 chops the defensive player after the contact by A2 has been broken and while A2 is still confronting the defensive player.

(9) On a kicking play, A1 chops a defensive player while A2 confronts the defensive player in a kick-blocking posture but is not physically engaged with the defensive player (a "lure").

(10) On a kicking play, A1 blocks a defensive player in the area of the thigh or lower, and A2, simultaneously or immediately after the block by A1, engages the defensive player high.

Note: Each of the above circumstances in subsections (7) through (10), which describes a chop-block foul on a kicking play, also applies on a play in which an offensive player indicates an apparent attempt to kick protect, but the play ultimately becomes a run.

Penalty: For Chop Block: Loss of 15 yards.

Section 3   UNSPORTSMANLIKE CONDUCT

Article 1   There shall be no unsportsmanlike conduct. This applies to any act which is contrary to the generally understood principles of sportsmanship. Such acts specifically include, among others:

(a) Throwing a punch, or a forearm, or kicking at an opponent even though no contact is made.

(b) The use of abusive, threatening, or insulting language or gestures to opponents, teammates, officials, or representatives of the League.

(c) The use of baiting or taunting acts or words that engender ill will between teams.

(d) Individual players involved in prolonged or excessive celebrations. Players are prohibited from engaging in any celebrations while on the ground. A celebration shall be deemed excessive or prolonged if a player continues to celebrate after a warning from anofficial.

(e) Two-or-more players engage in prolonged, excessive, premeditated, or choreographed celebrations.

(f) Possession or use of foreign or extraneous object(s) that are not part of the uniform during the game on the field or the sideline, or using the ball as a prop.

(g) Unnecessary physical contact with a game official.

(h) <u>Removal of his helmet by a player in the field of play during a celebration or during a confrontation with a game official or any other player.</u>

Note 1: Under no condition is an official to allow a player to shove, push, or strike him in an offensive, disrespectful, or unsportsmanlike manner. Any such action must be reported to the Commissioner.

Penalty: (for a through h): Loss of 15 yards from succeeding spot or whatever spot the Referee, after consulting with the crew, deems equitable.

Note 2: Violations of (b) or (c) (above), which occur before or during the game may result in disqualification in addition to the yardage penalty. Any violations at the game site on the day of the game, including postgame, may result in discipline by the Commissioner. Any violation of (g) (above) may result in disqualification and also will include discipline by the Commissioner. An official must see the entire action for a player to be disqualified.

Note 3: Violations of (b) will be penalized if any of the acts are committed directly at an opponent. These acts include but are not limited to: sack dances; home run swing; incredible hulk; spiking the ball; spinning the ball; throwing or shoving the ball; pointing; pointing the ball; verbal taunting; military salute; standing over an opponent (prolonged and with provocation); or dancing.

Note 4: Violations of (c) will be penalized if any of the acts occur anywhere on the field. These acts include but are not limited to: throat slash; machine gun salute; sexually suggestive gestures, prolonged gyrations; or stomping on a team logo.

Note 5: Violations of (d) will be penalized if they occur anywhere on the field other than the bench area.

Note 6: If any foreign object(s) are deemed a safety hazard by the game officials, in addition to a yardage penalty, the player will be subject to ejection from the game, whether he uses the object or not.

(i) The defensive use of acts or words designed to disconcert an offensive team at the snap. An official must blow his whistle immediately to stop play.

(j) Concealing a ball underneath the clothing or using any article of equipment to simulate a ball.

(k) Using entering substitutes, legally returning players, substitutes on sidelines, or withdrawn players to confuse opponents. The clarification is also to be interpreted as covering any lingering by players leaving the field when being substituted for. See 5-2-2.

(l) An offensive player lines up or is in motion less than five yards from the sideline in front of his team's designated bench area. However, an offensive player can line up less than five yards from the sidelines on the same side as his team's player bench, as long as he is not in front of the designated bench area.

(m) Repeatedly abusing the substitution rule (time in) in attempts to conserve time. See 5-2-2.

(n) More than two successive 40/25 second penalties (after warning) during same down.

(o) Jumping or standing on a teammate or opponent to block or attempt to block an opponent's kick.

(p) Placing a hand or hands on a teammate or opponent to gain additional height in the block or attempt to block an opponent's kick.

(q) Being picked up by a teammate in a block or an attempt to block an opponent's kick.

(r) Clearly running forward and leaping in an obvious attempt to block a field goal, or Try-kick after touchdown and landing on players, unless the leaping player was originally lined up within one yard of the line of scrimmage when the ball was snapped.

(s) Goal-tending by a defensive player leaping up to deflect a kick as it passes above the crossbar of a goalpost is prohibited. The Referee could award three points for a palpably unfair act (12-3-3).

(t) A punter, placekicker, or holder who simulates being roughed or run into by a defensive player.

(u) A member of the kicking team who goes out of bounds, whether forced out or voluntarily, <u>and does</u>

not attempt to return inbounds in a reasonable
amount of time.

(v) An attempt to call an excess or illegal timeout to
freeze a kicker prior to a field-goal attempt or a Try
attempt, when:
   (i) a team has already been charged a timeout
   during the same dead ball period; or
   (ii) a team has exhausted the three charged team
   timeouts that are permitted in a half.

If an attempt is made to call a timeout in these situations,
the officials shall not grant a timeout, play will continue,
and a penalty for unsportsmanlike conduct shall be
enforced. If a timeout is inadvertently granted, the
penalty shall also be enforced.

*Note: The Referee (or another official) will notify the Head
Coach (i) that two charged time outs by the same team in
the same dead ball period are not permitted, and (ii) when
he has exhausted his three charged team timeouts in a half.*

Penalty: For unsportsmanlike player conduct (i) through
(v): Loss of 15 yards from:

a) the succeeding spot if the ball is dead.

b) the previous spot if the ball was in play.

   If the infraction is flagrant, the player is also
   disqualified.

Article 2   The defense shall not commit successive or continued fouls
to prevent a score.

Penalty: For continuous fouls to prevent a score: If the violation is repeated after a warning, the score involved is
awarded to the offensive team.

Article 3   A player or substitute shall not interfere with play by any act which is palpably unfair.

Penalty: For a palpably unfair act: Offender may be disqualified. The Referee, after consulting his crew, enforces any such distance penalty as they consider equitable and irrespective of any other specified code penalty. The Referee could award a score. See 15-1-6.

Non-Player
Conduct

Rule 13

Non-Player Conduct

Section 1   NON-PLAYER CONDUCT

Article 1   There shall be no unsportsmanlike conduct by a substitute, coach, attendant, or any other non-player (entitled to sit on a team's bench) during any period or timeout (including between halves).

■ Supplemental Notes

(1) "Loud speaker" coaching from the sidelines is not permissible.

(2) A player may communicate with a coach provided the coach is in his prescribed area during dead ball periods.

Article 2   Either or both team attendants and their helpers may enter the field to attend their team during a team timeout by either team. No other non-player may come on the field without the Referee's permission, unless he is an incoming substitute (5-2-2).

Article 3   With the exception of uniformed players eligible to participate in the game, all persons in a team's bench area must wear a visible credential clearly marked "BENCH." For all NFL games—preseason, regular-season, and postseason—the home club will be issued a maximum of 27 credentials and the visiting club will be issued a maximum of 25 credentials for use in its bench area. Such credentials must be worn by coaches, players under contract to the applicable club but ineligible to participate in the game, and team support personnel (trainers, doctors, equipment men). From time to time, persons with game-services credentials (e.g., oxygen technicians, ball boys) and authorized club personnel not regularly assigned to the bench area may be in a team's bench area for a brief period without bench credentials. Clubs are prohibited from allowing into their bench areas any persons who are not officially affiliated with the club or otherwise serving a necessary game day function.

Article 4   All team personnel must observe the zone restrictions applicable to the bench area and the border rimming the playing field. The only persons permitted within the solid six-foot white border (1-1) while play is in progress on the field are game officials. For reasons involving the safety of participating players whose actions may carry them out of bounds, officials' unobstructed coverage of the game, and spectators' sightlines to the field, the border rules must be observed by all coaches and players in the bench area. Violators are subject to penalty by the officials.

Article 5   Coaches and other non-participating team personnel (including uniformed players not in the game at the time) are prohibited from moving laterally along the sidelines any further than the points that are 18 yards from the middle of the bench area (i.e., 32-yard lines to left and right of bench areas when benches are placed on opposite sides of the field). Lateral movement within the bench area must be behind the solid six-foot white border (see Article 4 above).

Article 6   Clubs are prohibited from allowing into the non-bench areas of field level any persons who have not been accredited to those locations by the home club's public-relations office for purposes related to news-media coverage, stadium operations, or pregame and halftime entertainment. The home club is responsible for keeping the field level cleared of all unauthorized persons. Photographers and other personnel accredited for field-level work must not be permitted in the end zones or any other part of the official playing field while play is in progress.

Penalty: For illegal acts under Articles 1 through 6 above: Loss of 15 yards from team for whose supposed benefit foul was made. (Unsportsmanlike conduct.)

Enforcement is from:

a) succeeding spot if the ball is dead.

b) whatever spot the Referee, after consulting with crew, deems equitable, if the ball was in play.

For a flagrant violation, the Referee may exclude offender or offenders from the playing field enclosure for the remainder of the game.

Article 7   A non-player shall not commit any act which is palpably unfair.

Penalty: For a palpably unfair act, see 12-3-3. The Referee, after consulting the crew, shall make such ruling as they consider equitable (15-1-6 and Note) (unsportsmanlike conduct).

Note: Various actions involving a palpably unfair act may arise during a game. In such cases, the officials may award a distance penalty in accordance with 12-3-3, even when it does not involve disqualification of a player or substitute. See 17-1.

Article 8   Non-player personnel of a club (e.g., management personnel, coaches, trainers, equipment men) are prohibited from making unnecessary physical contact with or directing abusive, threatening, or insulting language or gestures at opponents, game officials, or representatives of the League.

Penalty: Loss of 15 yards. (<u>Unsportsmanlike</u> conduct.) Enforcement is from:

a) succeeding spot if the ball is dead;

b) previous spot if the ball was in play; or

c) whatever spot the spot Referee, after consulting with the crew, deems equitable. (Palpably Unfair Act.)

Note: Violations which occur before or during the game may result in disqualification in addition to the yardage penalty. Any violation at the game site on the day of the game, including postgame, may result in discipline by the Commissioner.

Penalty
Enforcement

Rule 14

Penalty Enforcement

(Governing all cases not otherwise specifically provided for)

Section 1 SPOT FROM WHICH PENALTY IN FOUL IS ENFORCED

Article 1   The general provisions of Rule 14 govern all spots of enforcement.

Note: The spot of enforcement for fouls by players or the actual distance penalty or both, when not specific, are subordinate to the specific rules governing a foul during a fumble, pass or kick. These in turn are both subordinate to Rule 14.

A.R. 14.1 Second-and-15 on A4. Quarterback A1 throws a legal pass which is incomplete. A2 held in end zone.
Ruling: Safety or A's ball third-and-15 on A4.

Article 2   When a foul by a player occurs between downs, enforcement is from the succeeding spot (14-5-S.N. 3).

Article 3   Penalties for fouls committed by non-players shall be enforced as specifically provided under Rule 13.

Article 4   When the spot of enforcement is not governed by a general or specific rule, it is the spot of the foul.

Article 5   The basic spots of enforcement (3-11-1) are:

   (a) The previous spot for a forward pass (8-1-1); a scrimmage kick (9-5-1); or a free kick (6-4-1).

   (b) The dead ball spot on a running play (14-1-12).

   (c) The spot of snap, backward pass, or fumble (8-7).

   (d) The spot of the foul (14-1-4 and 14-1-13).

   (e) The succeeding spot for dead ball fouls. When such a foul by the defense incurs a penalty that results in the

offensive team being short of the previous spot, the
ball will be advanced to the previous spot.

*Note: If a foul is committed during a run, a fumble, or a
backward pass, the penalty is assessed from the basic spot if:*

    i)   Defense fouls in advance of the basic spot
   ii)   Defense fouls behind the basic spot
  iii)   Offense fouls in advance of the basic spot

If the offense fouls behind the basic spot, enforcement is
from the spot of the foul (3 and 1).

Exceptions:

1) All fouls committed by the offensive team behind the
line of scrimmage (except in the end zone) shall be
penalized from the previous spot. If the foul is in the
end zone, it is a safety (14-1-11-b).

2) If a runner (3-28-1) is downed behind the line of
scrimmage (except in the end zone) and the foul by
an offensive player is beyond the line of scrimmage,
enforcement shall be from the previous spot. If the
runner is down in the end zone, it is a safety
(11-5-1).

A.R. 14.2 Second-and-10 on A30. Runner A1 is
downed on the A35. Defensive B1 illegally uses his
hands on the A45 during run.
Ruling: The defensive foul is in advance of the basic
spot (A35 where downed). Penalize from the basic spot
(A35). A's ball first-and-10 on A40.

A.R. 14.3 Second-and-10 on A30. Runner A1 is
downed on the A35. Offensive player A2 uses his hands
illegally on the A45.
Ruling: The offensive foul is in advance of the basic spot
(A35 where downed). Penalize from the basic spot
(A35). A's ball second-and-15 on A25.

A.R. 14.4 Second-and-10 on A30. Runner A1 is downed on the A40. An offensive player illegally uses his hands on the A35.

Ruling: The offensive foul is behind the basic spot (spot where downed). Penalize from the spot of the foul (A35). A's ball second-and-15 on A25.

A.R. 14.5 Second-and-10 on A30. Quarterback A1 is downed on the A40. Offensive player A2 held on the A25.

Ruling: Penalize 10 yards from the previous spot as the offensive foul was behind the line of scrimmage. A's ball second-and-20 on A20.

A.R. 14.6 Second-and-10 on A30. Runner A1 is downed on the A25. An offensive player held on the A32.

Ruling: A's ball second-and-20 on the A20. The offensive runner was downed behind the line of scrimmage. Enforcement is from the previous spot. Team B has option of refusing the penalty and taking the play which would then be A's ball third-and-15 on the A25 (14-6).

Article 6   When the spot of a player foul is out of bounds between the end lines, it is assumed to be at an inbounds line on a yard line (extended) through the spot where the foul was committed. If this spot is behind an end line, it is assumed to be in the end zone. See 7-3-7 and 14-1-11.

Article 7   A dead ball foul is enforced from the succeeding spot, and the down counts.

> (a) If there is a dead ball personal foul by either team following the end of the second or fourth periods, the penalty yardage will be enforced on the second half kickoff or the kickoff in overtime.

A.R. 14.7 Second-and-10 on A30. Runner A1 goes out of bounds on the A35. Offensive player A2 then clips B1 either on the A40 or A30.

Ruling: Enforce from the succeeding spot (out of bounds) as a foul between downs. Dead ball foul. The down is counted as the foul occurred after the ball was dead from runner A1 going out of bounds. A's ball third-and-20 on A20.

A.R. 14.8 Fourth-and-10 on A30. A punt goes to the B30 where kicking team player A1 illegally touches the ball and then falls on it there, after which:

a) kicking team player A2 clips any place on the field.
   Ruling: B's ball first-and-10 on B45.

b) receiver B1 commits a personal foul any place on the field.
   Ruling: B's ball first-and-10 on B15.

A.R. 14.9 Fourth-and-8 on B12. A legal forward pass is incomplete behind the goal line. After the incompletion:

a) B1 knocks A1 to the ground.
   Ruling: Enforce from the succeeding spot (B12) as the pass was incomplete in the end zone on fourth down. B's ball first and-10 on B6.

b) A1 clips.
   Ruling: Enforce from the succeeding spot (B12). B's ball first-and-10 on B27.

Article 8   Dead ball fouls by both teams are offset at the succeeding spot and the down counts, except when one or both are disqualifying fouls, or as provided in 14-1-9. See 14-3-2.

A.R. 14.10 Fourth-and-5 on B14. A legal forward pass is incomplete behind the goal line, after which:

a) A1 clips B1 and B2 roughs A2.
   Ruling: Fouls are offset. They are dead ball fouls and the succeeding spot is B14. B's ball first-and-10 on B14.

b) A1 punches B1 and B1 punches A1.

Ruling: Dead ball fouls. Offsetting fouls; in addition, A1 and B1 are disqualified. B's ball first-and-10 on B14.

A.R. 14.11 Second-and-10 on A30. A legal forward pass is incomplete, after which:

a) B1 clips A1 and A1 punches B1.
   Ruling: Disqualify A1. Penalties offset. The down counts as the foul occurred after the down had ended. A's ball third-and-10 on A30. See 14-1-8.

b) A1 clips B1 and B1 punches A1.
   Ruling: Disqualify B1. Penalties offset. A's ball third-and-10 on A30.

A.R. 14.12 Receiver B1 is offside on the kickoff. The kickoff is legally out of bounds on the B30 (last touching a receiving team player) after which:

a) A1 is penalized for roughness.
   Ruling: Rekick. Double foul (14-3-2 and 14-1-9).

b) B1 is penalized for roughness.
   Ruling: Choice for Team A. Rekick from the A35 (offside penalty) or B's ball first- and-10 on B15. A dead ball foul is penalized from the succeeding spot (B30). If the kick is illegally out of bounds, it is a rekick in either case (14-4).

Article 9 If there has been a foul by either team during a down and there is a dead ball foul by the other team in the action immediately after the end of the down, it is a double foul, and all rules for enforcement of double fouls apply (see 14-3-1).

Exception: If the scoring team commits a dead ball foul after a score, the score counts, and the penalty is enforced on the kickoff.

A.R. 14.13 Second-and-10 on A30. Runner A1 is out of bounds on the A40, after which A2 clips any place.

Team B was offside.

Ruling: A's ball second-and-25 on A15. See 14-3-1-Exc. 1.

Article 10 There is no penalty unless the contact was avoidable and it is deemed unnecessary roughness, if a player:

(a) uses his hands, arms, or body in a manner ordinarily illegal (other than striking) during the dead ball period after a down ends, or

(b) completes a legal action (blocking or tackling) started during the down.

A.R. 14.14 Second-and-10 on A30. Runner A1 goes out of bounds on the A35 after which:

a) offensive A2 holds on the A30.
Ruling: Ignore the foul as it was illegal use of hands and not a personal foul. A's ball third-and-5 on A35.

b) offensive A2 clips on the A30.
Ruling: A personal foul during a dead ball is penalized as stated in 14-1-7. A's ball third-and-20 on A20.

c) offensive A2 strikes B1 on the A30.
Ruling: Disqualify A2. Penalize from the succeeding spot as in 14-1-7. A's ball third-and-20 on A20.

Article 11 When a spot of enforcement is behind the offensive goal line, and the foul is:

(a) by the defense, a distance penalty is measured from the goal line (unless a touchback, one during a backward pass, or fumble, or

(b) by the offense, it is a safety.

Note: During a loose ball there is always an offensive and defensive team, and enforcement is provided for in the specific section governing passes, fumbles, and kicks. See 3-2-3; 3-17; 3-36-1; and 14-1-5.

A.R. 14.15 Receiver B1 fumbles after catching a punt on his 1-yard line. The ball enters the end zone where B1 recovers. During a run in the end zone, he fumbles. A1 clips anywhere during the last fumble. B1 is downed in the end zone.
Ruling: Enforce from the goal line. B's ball first-and-10 on B15.

A.R. 14.16 Second-and-15 on A4. Runner A1 is downed in the end zone. During the run A2 held on the A10.
Ruling: Safety. Decline penalty.

A.R. 14.17 Second-and-goal on B2. Runner A1 fumbles into B's end zone. B1 recovers in his end zone (downed) or goes out of bounds from there. While B1 is a runner, B2 fouls in the end zone.
Ruling: Safety.

Article 12 When a foul occurs during a running play (3-28-2) and the run in which the foul occurs is not followed by a change of team possession during the down, the spot of enforcement is the spot where the ball is dead.

Exceptions:

1) When the spot of a foul by the offense is behind the spot where dead, enforcement is from the spot of the foul.

2) When the spot of a foul by the offense is behind the line of scrimmage, enforcement is from the previous spot unless in offensive's end zone. Then it is a safety (14-1-11-b).

3) When the spot of a foul by the offense is beyond the line of scrimmage and a runner (3-28-1) is downed behind the line, enforcement is from the previous spot unless he is downed in the end zone. Then it is a safety, the result of the play (11-5-1).

4) When the spot of a foul is that of an illegal forward pass, enforcement is from the spot of the pass. This does not apply to a second forward pass from behind the line, or a forward pass from behind the line after the ball had been beyond the line, which is enforced from the previous spot, unless the spot of the pass is behind the passer's goal line. See 14-1-11-b.

5) If the spot of a defensive foul occurs on or beyond the line of scrimmage and the ball becomes dead behind the line, penalty is enforced from the previous spot.

6) When the spot of enforcement for the defense is behind the offensive goal line, enforcement is from the goal line. See 14-1-11-a.

7) When the spot of a foul by the defense is behind the line of scrimmage and the ball becomes dead behind the line, enforcement is from the spot of the foul or the spot where the ball is dead, whichever is more advantageous to the offense. If such foul incurs a penalty that results in the offended team being short of the line, the ball will be advanced to the previous spot and no additional yardage assessed.

A.R. 14.18 While B1 is returning a kickoff, B2 holds on the B30. B1 is downed on the B20.
Ruling: The offensive foul is in advance of the dead ball; enforce from the dead ball spot (B20). First-and-10 on B10.

Article 13 When a defensive foul occurs during a running play (3-28-2) and the run in which the foul occurs is followed by a change of possession, the spot of enforcement is the spot of the foul and ball reverts to offensive team. See 14-1-12- Exc. 5.

Exceptions:

1) When the spot of a foul is in advance of the spot where the offensive player lost possession, the spot of

---

enforcement is the spot where player possession was
lost and the ball reverts to offensive team.

2) When the spot of a foul by the defense is at, behind,
or beyond the line of scrimmage, and such foul
incurs a penalty that results in the offensive team
being short of the line, the ball will be advanced to
the previous spot.

*Note: When there are multiple fouls by the defense, enforce-
ment should benefit the offense the most.*

A.R. 14.19 Second-and-10 on A30. Runner A1 goes to
the A40 where he fumbles and B1 recovers. During A1's
run, B2 held on the line of scrimmage (A30).
Ruling: Penalize from the spot of the foul on change of
possession. A's ball first-and-10 on A35.

A.R. 14.20 Second-and-10 on A30. Runner A1 goes to
the A40 where he fumbles and B1 recovers. During A1's
run, B2 held on the A45.
Ruling: Enforce from the spot where the offensive player
A1 lost possession as the foul was in advance of where
player A1 lost possession. If Team A had been the only
one to foul, Team B would refuse the penalty and keep
the ball. A's ball first-and-10 on A45.

A.R. 14.21 Second-and-10 on A30. Quarterback A1
scrambles to A20, fumbles and B1 recovers. During A1's
scramble, B2 holds at A22.
Ruling: A's ball first-and-10 on A30. See 14-1-13-Exc. 2.

■ Supplemental Notes

(1) A foul during a run prior to a kick or forward pass
from behind the line, is enforced as if it had occurred
during a pass or kick which follows. See 8-6-1; 8-6-2;
8-6-3; 9-5-1; and 14-1-5.

(2) If an offensive player fouls behind the defensive goal line during a running play in which the runner crosses that line, the penalty is enforced from the spot where the runner crossed the goal line.

(3) After a penalty for a foul during a running play, the general provisions of 14-8-1 relative to the number of the ensuing down, always apply.

(4) Any foul prior to possession by a runner is enforced as otherwise specified.

A.R. 14.22 Second-and-10 on A30. Runner A1 crosses the goal line. During A1's run:

a) A2 clips on the B20.
   Ruling: Enforce from the spot of the foul. A's ball first-and-10 on B35.

b) A2 clips in B's end zone before Runner A1 crosses the goal line.
   Ruling: Enforcement is from the goal line. A's ball first-and-10 on B15.

c) A2 clips on the B10 after Runner A1 crosses the goal line.
   Ruling: Touchdown. Kickoff on A15.

Article 14 If a team scores and the opponent commits a personal or unsportsmanlike conduct foul or a palpably unfair act during the down, the penalty is enforced on the succeeding free kick unless the enforcement resulted in the score.

Note: If the personal foul, unsportsmanlike conduct foul, or a palpably unfair act by the opponent occurred on a successful field goal or Try kick, the penalty could be enforced from the previous spot and the offensive team would retain the ball, with no score.

A.R. 14.23 Second-and-10 on B30. A legal forward pass is caught by end A1 who then runs for a score. Prior to the pass B1 holds A2 on the line of scrimmage.
Ruling: Touchdown. Kickoff on A30. No enforcement of penalty as it was not a personal foul but defensive holding.

A.R. 14.24 Second-and-15 on A2. Runner A1 is downed in the end zone. A2 clipped in the end zone during the run.
Ruling: Safety. Free kick from A10. The personal foul is penalized from the succeeding spot (A20) as the foul did not result in a score.

A.R. 14.25 B1 clips during a kickoff. B1 muffs the kick on the B5 and forces it into his end zone (new impetus) where he recovers and is downed or the kick is out of bounds from the end zone.
Ruling: Safety. Team B free kicks from its 10 as the penalty is also enforced for the clip from the succeeding spot (B20).

A.R. 14.26 Second-and-12 on A4. Runner A1 fumbles in his end zone, where B1 recovers. During A's run:

a) A2 holds anywhere.
   Ruling: Touchdown Team B. Kickoff at B30.

b) B2 holds anywhere.
   Ruling: Enforce from the goal line. A's ball first-and-10 on A5 (14-1-13).

A.R. 14.27 During a successful Try-kick, B1:

a) is offside.
   Ruling: Point awarded. Enforce five-yard penalty against B on kickoff (See 11-3-3) or retry at B1.

b) piles on holder of a placekick or runs into the kicker.
   Ruling: Point awarded. Enforce the penalty on the succeeding kickoff (11-3-3-c) or retry at B1.

Section 2   **LOCATION OF FOUL**

Article 1   If a distance penalty, enforced from a specific spot
between the goal lines would place the ball more than half
the distance to the offender's goal line, the penalty shall be
half the distance from that spot to their goal line.

*Note: This general rule supersedes any other general or spe-
cific rule other than for a palpably unfair act or the enforcement for intentional grounding, if appropriate.*

A.R. 14.28 Second-and-20 on B24. A legal forward pass
is caught by end A1 on the B12 and he runs to the B10.
B1 roughed the passer.
Ruling: Half the distance from the end of the run. A's
ball first-and-goal on B5.

Article 2   (a) If a foul occurs behind a goal line during a down, the
penalty shall be enforced as provided for under the
specific running play, pass or fumble rule involved.

(b) If a foul occurs between downs, enforcement is from
the succeeding spot (14-5).

(c) If any enforcement leaves or places the ball behind a
goal line, 11-3-5 and 11-3-6 govern. See 14-1-11
and Note.

Section 3   **FOULS BY BOTH TEAMS**

Article 1   If there is a double foul (3-11-2-c) without a change of
possession, the penalties are offset and the down is
replayed at the previous spot. If it was a scrimmage
down, the number of the next down and the necessary
line is the same as for the down for which the new one is
substituted.

Exceptions:

1) If one of the fouls is of a nature that incurs a 15-yard
penalty and the other foul of a double foul normally

would result in a loss of 5 yards *only* (15 yards versus 5 yards), the major penalty yardage is to be assessed from the previous spot.

Note: If a score occurs on a play that would normally involve a 5 vs. 15 yard enforcement, enforce the major penalty from the previous spot.

2) If one of the fouls is a dead ball foul for delay of game for spiking the ball and the opponent's foul is a live ball foul, the team that committed the delay of game foul, in addition to Article 1 and Exception 1, will have the option to decline the foul committed by its opponent and be assessed the penalty for delay from the dead ball spot.

3) Any disqualified player is removed immediately, even when one or both fouls are disqualifying or are disregarded otherwise. See 14-1-8.

4) If both fouls involve disqualification, the down is replayed at the previous spot. If both fouls are dead ball fouls or are treated as such (14-1-8), the fouls are disregarded and the ball is next put in play at the succeeding spot. See Exception 1 in either case.

5) If the one foul by the kickers during a down is illegal touching of a scrimmage kick, the down is not replayed at the previous spot. The foul (illegal touching) by the kickers is disregarded provided the distance penalty for a foul by the receivers is enforced. If not enforced, the receivers next put the ball in play at any spot of illegal touching or at any other spot where they are entitled to possession at the end of the down. However, a postpossession foul cannot be declined in order to force B's possession at any spot of illegal touching (9-5-1-Exc. 2).

Note: Any foul by either team after a kick ends is enforced as ordinary. See 9-5-1.

A.R. 14.29 Second-and-20 on A30. Runner A1 goes to the A35. During the run A2 holds B1 who punches A2. **Ruling:** Disqualify B1. Penalties offset. A's ball second-and-20 on A30.

A.R. 14.30 Third-and-eight on B10. A2 is offside and B1 slugs on the B6 during the play. Runner A1 scored on the play.
Ruling: Disqualify B1. A's ball first-and-goal on B5.

A.R. 14.31 Second-and-10 on A30. B1 is offside. Runner A1 goes to B30. During A's run A2 clips at the 50.
Ruling: A's ball second-and-25 on A15. See 14-3-1-Exc. 1.

A.R. 14.32 Second-and-10 on A30. After the ball is dead anywhere, A1 and B2 strike each other with their fists. Runner A1 was downed on the A35.
Ruling: Fouls are disregarded except for disqualifying both players. A's ball third-and-five on A35.

A.R. 14.33 Fourth-and-10 on B18. A forward pass falls incomplete in the end zone, after which A1 clips B2 who then strikes A1.
Ruling: Disqualify B2. B's ball first-and-10 on B18.

A.R. 14.34 A kickoff is illegally out of bounds on the B30. After the ball is out of bounds:

a) A1 clips and B2 blocks below the waist.
   Ruling: B's ball first-and-10 on B40.

b) A1 clips and B1 punches A1.
   Ruling: B's ball first-and-10 on B40. B1 disqualified.

Article 2   If there is a double foul (3-11-2-c) during a down in which there is a change of possession, the team gaining possession must keep the ball after enforcement for its foul, provided its foul occurred after the change of possession (clean hands).

Exceptions:

1) If the kickers foul during a kickoff, punt, safety kick, or field-goal attempt before possession changes, the receivers will have the option of replaying the down at the previous spot (offsetting fouls), or keeping the ball after enforcement for its fouls.

2) If the team gaining possession fouls and loses possession, the penalties offset and the down is replayed at the previous spot.

3) If a score would result from a foul by a team gaining possession, the down is replayed at the previous spot.

If the team gaining possession fouls prior to the change of possession (not clean hands), the penalties offset and the down is replayed at the previous spot.

Article 3   If a double foul occurs after a change in possession, the team in possession retains the ball at the spot where the team in possession's foul occurred so long as that spot is not in advance of the dead ball spot. In that event, ball is spotted at dead ball spot.

(a) If this spot is normally a touchback, the ball is placed on the 20-yard line.

(b) If normally a safety, place the ball on 1-yard line.

(c) This enforcement also applies if one of the fouls is a post-possession foul.

(d) If there is a subsequent change of possession (e.g., fumble recovery) after the double foul, and the foul by the team in possession is in advance of the spot of the fumble, the ball is put in play by the fumbling team at the spot of the fumble.

(e) If the foul by the team in possession is a dead ball foul, the ball is put in play at the dead ball spot.

■ Supplemental Notes

(1) When enforcement for a double foul is disregarded, the number of the next down, if a scrimmage down, is the same as if no foul had occurred. See 14-3-3.

(2) Change of possession refers to the physical change of possession from one team to the other except for kicks from scrimmage (9-5-1), and free kick.

(3) If a team fouls before it gains possession on a double foul, it cannot score.

(4) Illegal touching of a scrimmage kick, while technically a foul, does not offset a foul committed by its opponent. It is not considered part of a double foul. See 14-3-1-Exc. 5.

A.R. 14.35 Second-and-10 on B40. B2 is offside and A1 completes a pass to eligible receiver A3 who is tackled at the B17. A3 then gets up and spikes the ball in the field of play.
Ruling: A's ball first-and-10 on B22 (decline B's foul and enforce A's from dead-ball spot).

A.R. 14.36 Second-and-10 on B40. Offensive Team A is offside. B1 intercepts a forward pass and runs it back to the A30. On the runback, B2 clips on the B45.
Ruling: Team B keeps the ball as its foul was not prior to change of possession and foul enforced. B's ball first-and-10 on B30.

A.R. 14.37 On the kickoff to start the game, kicking team player A1 is offside. Receiver B1 catches the ball in the end zone and runs it back to the A20. On the runback B2 clips on the A26.

Ruling: B's ball first-and-10 on A41 (14-3-2).

A.R. 14.38 Fourth-and-10 on A40. Kicking team player A1 is offside. A punt hits on the B20 where receiver B1 picks it up and runs to the 50. On B's runback, B2 clips on the B40.

Ruling: B's ball first-and-10 on B25 (14-3-2).

A.R. 14.39 Fourth-and-10 on A40. Kicking team player A1 is offside. A punt hits on the B20 where receiver B1 picks it up and runs for a touchdown. After B1 scores, B2 clips on the A10.

Ruling: Touchdown Team B. Kickoff B15 (14-3-2).

A.R. 14.40 Second-and-five on B45. Team A is offside. B1 intercepts a pass on the B10 and runs it back to the B30 and is tackled and fumbles on the B30 where A1 recovers. On B1's run, B2 clipped on the B25.

Ruling: A's ball second-and-5 on B45 (14-3-2).

A.R. 14.41 Second-and-10 on A30. Team A is offside. B1 intercepts and runs for a touchdown, then clips.

Ruling: Touchdown Team B. Kickoff B15.

A.R. 14.42 Second-and-10 on B45. B1 intercepts a pass on the B10 and runs it back to the A30. On the runback, B2 clips on the A35 and A1 piles on runner B1 after as he is tackled on the A30.

Ruling: Team B retains ball at spot of its foul. B's ball first-and-10 on A35.

A.R. 14.43 B1 receives a kick at the B10, advances to the B40 and fumbles when he is tackled. A2 recovers. During B1's run, B2 clips at the B30, after which A1 trips B3.

Ruling: Double foul following change of possession. B's ball at spot of its foul, first- and-10 on B30.

A.R. 14.44 Defensive B1 intercepts on the B10. During B1's run, B2 clips at the B30 and is downed at the B40. B1 is flagrantly roughed by A1 who piles on.
Ruling: A1 disqualified. B's ball first-and-10 on B30.

A.R. 14.45 Second-and-10 on B45. B1 holds tight end A1 on the line of scrimmage. B2 intercepts the ball on the B10 and runs it back to the B30 where he is tackled, fumbles, and A2 recovers the ball. A2 runs to the B20. On A2's run, A3 holds on the B25.
Ruling: Team A keeps the ball as it gained possession prior to its foul. A's ball first-and-10 on B35.

A.R. 14.46 B1 receives a kickoff in the end zone and clips there. The runner advances to the B25 and is piled on by A1.
Ruling: B's ball first-and-10 on B1. See 14-3-3-b.

A.R. 14.47 B1 legally bats a kickoff back into his own end zone, thereby creating a new impetus. After B3 picks up the ball in the end zone, B2 clips in the end zone and A1 piles on.
Ruling: Both fouls occurred after Team B gained possession. Normally, if this spot was in the end zone, the succeeding spot would be the B20. In this case, B1 created the impetus which would have resulted in a safety if the fouls had not been committed. The ball is transferred to the one-yard line. B's ball first-and-10 on B1. See 14-3-3-b.

A.R. 14.48 Second-and-10 on B30. Offensive A1 offside. B1 intercepts in the end zone and clips there. Runner B1 is downed on the B10.
Ruling: Replay. A score cannot result from one of the fouls of a double foul. A's ball second-and-10 on B30. Sec 14-3-2.

Section 4   **CHOICE OF PENALTIES**

If there is a multiple foul (3-11-2-b) by the same team during the same down, only one penalty may be enforced after the Referee has explained the alternatives. The captain of the offended team shall make the choice.

Exception 1: If one of the multiple fouls is a foul against a game official, then both fouls are enforced.

Exception 2: If the defensive team commits a personal foul that is also pass interference, then both fouls are enforced.

Note: A disqualified player is always removed, regardless of any captain's choice. See 5-1-3.

A.R. 14.49 Second-and-10 on A30. Runner A1 goes to the A35. During the run, A2 clipped on the A30. Team A was offside.
Ruling: A multiple foul and only one penalty can be enforced. Option for defensive Team B. A's ball second-and-15 on A25 or A's ball second-and-25 on A15. If both declined, it is third-and-five on A35.

A.R. 14.50 B1 makes an invalid fair catch signal at the B20. The ball goes over his head, lands at the B3-yard line and bounces into the end zone. Before the ball went into the end zone B1 blocked A4 at the B22.
Ruling: Multiple fouls but only one can be enforced. Option for Team A. B's ball first-and-10 on B11 or B's ball first-and-10 on B15.

A.R. 14.51 B1 intercepts a pass in the end zone. He runs and is downed in the end zone. B2 holds in the end zone during B1's run. B3 clips after the ball is dead.
Ruling: If the penalty for holding is declined, it is Team B on its 10 (touchback minus 10). If the penalty for holding is enforced (which it would be), it is a safety and Team B free kicks from its 10 (14-1-14).

A.R. 14.52 B1 fumbles after catching a punt on his 2-yard line. In attempting to recover in the end zone, he deliberately kicks the ball out of bounds behind the goal line.

a) B2 clips on his 4 during the fumble.
   Ruling: If Team A accepts the penalty for clipping, it is B's ball on its one-yard line. Otherwise, it is a safety. Safety kick from B10.

b) B2 clips on his 4 after the ball is out of bounds.
   Ruling: Safety. Team B free kicks from its 10 (14-1-14).

Section 5 **TIME OF FOUL**

If a foul occurs between downs (3-11-2-a), a distance penalty is enforced from the succeeding spot. See 14-1-7 to 14-1-10.

A.R. 14.53 Second-and 10 on A31. Quarterback A1 completes a pass to end A3 at the A45. Tackle A6 and back A2 chop blocked B5 at the A28. After the play, A6 grabbed the Referee to argue the call.
Ruling: Both fouled enforced. A's ball second-and-33 on A8.

A.R. 14.54 Second-and-10 on A30. Runner A1 goes out of bounds on the A35, after which offensive player A2 clips on the A30.
Ruling: The down counts and enforce from the succeeding spot (A35)(14-1-5-b and 14-1-7). A's ball third-and-20 on A20.

A.R. 14.55 Third-and-five on A30. Offensive team is offside and runner A1 fails to gain. A2 clips just before the ball is declared dead.
Ruling: If defensive Team B declines both penalties, it is fourth-and-five on the A30. If the penalty for clipping is enforced, it is third-and-20 on A15.

A.R. 14.56 Fourth-and-10 on A40. Kicking team player A1 first touches and recovers a scrimmage kick on the B10:

a) after an illegal recovery by A1, A2 roughs an opponent.
   Ruling: B's ball first-and-10 on B25.

b) after an illegal recovery by A1, B2 roughs an opponent.
   Ruling: B's ball first-and-10 on B5.

■ **Supplemental Notes**

(1) When a foul occurs simultaneously with an out of bounds or after a loose ball crosses the plane of the boundary line in the air and then first touches anything out of bounds, it is considered to be a dead ball foul.

(2) The succeeding spot for a foul after a touchdown and before a whistle for a Try is the next kickoff (3-11-1-Exc.).

(3) The time between downs is the interval during all time outs (including intermissions) and from the time the ball is dead until it is next put in play (time in). See 3-37-1, 3-37-2.

(4) For a dead ball foul by the defensive team or by either team at the end of a play not from scrimmage, see 14-8-6.

(5) See 5-1-8-S.N. for a special enforcement between downs.

A.R. 14.57 Third-and-20 on B40. Runner A1 is out of bounds on the B15, after which offensive player A2 clips on the B20.
Ruling: Team A had made its first down, and as it was a dead ball foul, enforce from the succeeding spot (14-1-7). A's ball first-and-10 on B30.

A.R. 14.58 Third-and-10 on B30. A forward pass is out of bounds on the B10 after which A1 clips on B15.
Ruling: A's ball fourth-and-25 on B45.

A.R. 14.59 Offensive Team A has made a first down and its captain calls time out for the fourth time in the half without making a substitution for an injured player.
Ruling: A's ball first-and-10. Deny request.

A.R. 14.60 Receiver B1 catches a punt on the B30 and goes out of bounds on the B40, after which B2 clips on the B35.
Ruling: Dead ball foul (14-1-7). B's ball first-and-10 on B25. Also see 14-8-6.

A.R. 14.61 Second-and-15 on A30. Runner A1 steps out of bounds on A40, after which A2 clips on 50.
Ruling: Enforce from the dead ball spot (A40)(14-1-7). A's ball third-and-20 on A25.

A.R. 14.62 Second-and-15 on A30. Runner A1 steps out of bounds on the 50, after which A2 clips on A40.
Ruling: A's ball first-and-10 on A35 (14-1-7).

Section 6 **REFUSAL OF PENALTIES**

Penalties for all fouls, unless otherwise expressly provided for, may be declined by the Captain of the offended team, in which case play proceeds as though no foul had been committed.

Note: The yardage distance for any penalty may be declined, even though the penalty is accepted.

A.R. 14.63 Second-and-10 on A30. A legal forward pass is completed to end A1 on the A45 where he is downed. Defensive B1 held flanker A2 on the A35 prior to the pass.
Ruling: Declines holding penalty which would have

---

been five yards from the previous spot and a first down. A's ball first-and-10 on A45.

Exceptions:

1) A disqualified or suspended player is always removed, even when an accompanying distance penalty is declined, or when a penalty for another foul is chosen (multiple foul).

2) During a down a foul occurs for which the ball is dead immediately.

3) The penalty for certain illegal actions prior to or pertaining to a snap or to a free kick may not be declined, i.e., the ball remains dead.
   a) 40/25-second violations (4-6-1 and 4-6-2).
   b) Snap made before the officials can assume their normal stance (7-3-3-c-2).

4) When a 40/25-second penalty occurs prior to the snap, the defensive team may decline a distance penalty, in which case the down is replayed from the previous spot.

5) If fouls are committed by both teams during the same down (double foul), no penalty may be declined, except as provided for kickers when their only foul is illegal touching of a scrimmage kick. See 14-3-1-Exc. 5.

6) If the defensive team commits a foul during an unsuccessful Try, the offensive team may decline the distance penalty and the down is replayed from the previous spot.

A.R. 14.64 Second-and-10 on A30. On a legal forward pass B1 interferes with eligible A1 on the B40 where the ball falls incomplete. B2 strikes A2 on the line of scrimmage.

Ruling: Disqualify B2 although the penalty for interference is taken. A's ball first-and-10 on B40.

A.R. 14.65 During time in, A1 illegally recovers a kick, unduly advances, and fumbles. B2 recovers and advances beyond the spot where the penalty for delay by A1 would place the ball.
Ruling: B's ball at the spot of A's illegal recovery.

Section 7   **ON INCOMPLETE FORWARD PASS**

An illegal forward pass is a foul, but an incomplete forward pass is not classed as a foul and the penalties provided therefore may not be declined.

Note: If there is a dead ball foul by either team after an incompletion, enforcement is from the succeeding spot. See 14-5.

Section 8   **NUMBER OF DOWN AFTER PENALTY**

Article 1   After a distance penalty (not combined with a loss-of-down penalty) for a foul by the offensive team prior to (between downs) or during a play from scrimmage which results in the ball being in its possession behind the necessary line, the number of the ensuing down is the same as that of the down before which or during which the foul occurred.

Article 2   A combination penalty involving both distance and loss of down is enforced for certain forward pass fouls by the offensive team.

Examples:

(a) from beyond the line (8-1-2-Pen. a); or

(b) intentionally grounded (8-2-1).

Note: After a loss-of-down penalty (prior to fourth down), the number of the ensuing down is one greater than that of

*the previous down. If it occurs on fourth down, it is loss of
the ball to the defensive team unless it is a combination
penalty, in which case the distance penalty is enforced in
addition to the loss of the ball.*

Article 3 When a foul occurs during a play from scrimmage, the
necessary line remains the same regardless of any change of
team possession thereafter.

A.R. 14.66 Second-and-10 on A30. Team A is offside. A
legal forward pass is intercepted by defensive B1 on the
50. B1 runs to the A40, fumbles, and A2 recovers there.
Ruling: A's ball second-and-15 on A25. (If Team B
refused the penalty, it would have been A's ball first-
and-10 on A40).

Article 4 After a distance penalty for a foul by the offensive team
during a play from scrimmage which results in the ball
being in advance of the necessary line, it is a first-and-10 for
the offensive team.

Articles 4 and 6 also apply to a dead ball foul of the
offensive team at the end of a play from scrimmage
during which it has been constantly in possession.

A.R. 14.67 Second-and-4 on A30. Runner A1 goes to
the B45. During the run, A2 clipped on the 50.
Ruling: After the penalty, the ball is still in advance of
the necessary line for the first down. A's ball first-and-10
on A35.

Article 5 After a penalty for a foul by the defense prior to (between
downs) or during a play from scrimmage, the ensuing
down is first-and-10 for the offense.

Exceptions are:

1) offside;

2) encroachment;

3) neutral zone infraction;

4) delay of game;

5) illegal substitution;

6) excess timeout;

7) running into kicker; and

8) more than 11 players on the field at the snap.

In the above eight exceptions the number of the down and the necessary line remain the same unless a distance penalty places the ball on or in advance of that line, in which case it is first-and-10 for Team A.

A.R. 14.68 Second-and-15 on A30. Runner A1 is downed on the A35. During the run defensive B1 held on the line of scrimmage.
Ruling: A's ball first-and-10 on A40.

A.R. 14.69 Third-and-goal on B4. The defensive team is offside and A1 gains one yard.
Ruling: A's ball third-and-goal on the B2 (14-2-1).

Article 6   After a distance penalty for a foul which occurs during a play after team possession has changed following a snap or free kick, it is first-and-10 for the team that was in possession at the time of the foul or at the time of the dead ball foul.

A.R. 14.70 On a kickoff B1 runs to the B45 where he steps out of bounds, after which B2 clips on the 50.
Ruling: B's ball first-and-10 on B30.

Article 7   After a loss of ball penalty, it is first-and-10 for the offended team after enforcement, unless the offended team free kicks following the fair catch interference.

Note: Loss of ball results only from illegal touching of kick (other than a free kick) or a fair catch interference. See 6-1-4 and 10-1-1.

A.R. 14.71 Second-and-10 on A30. B1 intercepts a legal forward pass on the A40. He fumbles and A1 recovers on the A25. A1 runs to the A45. During A1's run A2 clipped on the 50.

Ruling: A's ball first-and-10 on A30 (change of possession).

Officials: Jurisdiction and Duties

Rule 15

Officials: Jurisdiction and Duties

Section 1   **OFFICIALS**

Article 1   By League action, the officials' manual is an integral part of the Official rules, especially in regard to the specific duties, mechanics and procedures for each official during any play situations. For that reason, many such specific items are omitted in Sections 1 to 8 to avoid needless repetition, and only the primary duties of each official are stated. Some of the technical terms used hereafter are defined only in the manual.

Note: The terms "On Ball" or "Cover" imply that an official is nearest or in close proximity to a loose ball or runner and is in position to declare the ball dead when the down ends by rule. See 15-1-11-S.N. 1-3.

Article 2   The game Officials are: Referee, Umpire, Head Linesman, Line Judge, Field Judge, Side Judge, and Back Judge.

Note: In the absence of seven officials, the crew is to be rearranged, on the most feasible basis, according to the other members of crew.

Article 3   All officials are to wear uniforms prescribed by the League (including a black cap with visor and piping for all except the Referee, who will wear a white cap). All officials will carry a whistle and a weighted bright gold flag.

Article 4   An official is to blow his whistle:

(a) for any foul for which ball remains dead or is dead immediately;

(b) to signal timeout at end of a down, during which he has indicated a foul, by means of dropping his flag

and provided no other official <u>signaled</u> timeout at
end of down;

(c) to indicate dead ball when he is covering a runner.
See 7-4-1, 2, 3, 4, 5.

(d) at any other time, when he is nearest to ball, when a
down ends. See 15-8-3.

*Note: The flag is to be used to indicate a foul. See 7-4-5-
Note.*

Article 5 Members of the crew are required to meet in their dressing
quarters at least 2 hours and 15 minutes before game time.

*Note: By order of the Commissioner, from the time any offi-
cial first enters the dressing room, and until all officials
have left it at the end of the game, no person other than
clubhouse attendants or those invited by the Referee shall be
allowed to enter it. This prohibition includes coaches,
players, owners, and other management personnel.*

Article 6 All officials are responsible for any decision involving the
application of a rule, its interpretation or an enforcement.
If an official errs in his interpretation of a rule, the other
officials must check him before play is resumed, otherwise
they are equally responsible. In the event of a disagreement,
the crew should draw aside for a conference.

*Note: If because of injury, the officials' vote is tied, Referee's
decision will be the deciding factor. Any dissenting opinion
is to be reported to the supervisor.*

Article 7 All officials have concurrent jurisdiction over any foul, and
there is no fixed territorial division in this respect. When an
official signals a foul, he must report it to the Referee,
informing him of its nature, position of ball at time of
foul, the offender (when known), the penalty and spot of
enforcement.

Article 8   Each official is to record every foul he signals and the total number of officials signalling the same foul. During the game, these are to be recorded on game cards provided by league. They are to be preserved after each game in case they should be needed to revise an official's final game card.

Article 9   At the end of the game the officials are to record their own fouls on game cards provided by the league, and are to check them with other officials, for duplications, before leaving the dressing room.

Note: Game cards are to be made out in accordance with the yearly bulletin issued for that purpose.

Article 10   All members of a crew are equally responsible for any errors in Officiating Mechanics as prescribed by the Manual, and are required to call the attention of this fact to an official who had been remiss.

Note: This applies to such errors, in mechanics or applications of rules, as tend to increase the length of the game (elapsed time) and particularly so to those which result in undue loss of playing time (Crew Time). In the latter case, if the Referee has clearly failed to signal a Referee's time out as specified by rule, any official should do so. See 4-5-5 and 4-5-6.

Article 11   Ten minutes before the opening kickoff, the entire crew is to appear on the field. Three minutes prior to the kickoff the Referee is to make the toss of the coin. He is to indicate which team is to receive and is to do the same when teams first appear on the field prior to the start of the second half. See 4-2-2.

Note: All officials record results of coin toss and options chosen.

■ **Supplemental Notes**

(1) During any running play (includes runbacks), or a loose ball, the nearest official is to cover and remain

with the ball or runner, unless outdistanced until end
of down. In such case any nearer official is to cover.
See 15-2-9-Note, for Referee entering a side zone
and 15-3-4 for Umpire.

(2) When a ball is dead inbounds near a sideline, during
time in, the official covering is to use the clock signal
to indicate this fact.

(3) Any officials not involved in an enforcement are to
see that all players other than captains remain aside
during any conference between Referee and captains.
See 15-2-5.

Article 12   All officials must record charged team timeouts.

Section 2   **REFEREE**

Article 1   The Referee is to have general oversight and control of
game. He is the final authority for the score, and the
number of a down in case of a disagreement. His
decisions upon all matters not specifically placed under
the jurisdiction of other officials, either by rule or the
officials' manual, are to be final. See 15-1-6-Note and
15-1-10.

Article 2   Prior to the kickoff to start each half and after every
timeout, the Referee shall sound his whistle for play to
start without asking captains if they are ready. In such cases
where time is in with his whistle, he is to indicate it by use
of clock signal.

Article 3   He is to see that the ball is properly put in play and shall
decide on all matters pertaining to its position and dispo-
sition at end of down. If any official sounds his whistle,
the ball is dead (7-4-1). In case the Referee is informed or
believes that ball was dead before such signal or down ends,
he has the authority to make a retroactive ruling after consulting the crew or the official involved.

Article 4   The Referee must notify the coach and field captain when his team has used its three charged time outs, signal both coaches when two minutes remain in a half, and positively inform the coach of any disqualified player. He may not delegate any such notifications to any other person. He will announce on the microphone when each period is ended.

Article 5   After a foul, the Referee (in the presence of both captains) must announce the penalty and explain to the offended captain the decision and choice (if any) as well as number of next down and distance (usually approximate) to necessary line for any possible positions of ball. See 7-1-2. The Referee is to designate the offending player, when known. After an enforcement (7-3-2) he shall signal to spectators the nature of penalty by means of the visual signals specifically provided for herein.

Note: It is not necessary for the Referee to explain to both captains the decision and distance to the necessary line in such cases when: the enforcement is entirely automatic and/or when there is obviously no choice.

Field captains only may appeal to Referee, and then solely on questions of interpretation of the rules. They shall not be allowed to question the judgment or jurisdiction of any particular official in regard to a foul or in <u>signaling</u> dead ball.

Article 6   Prior to the snap, the Referee shall assume such a stance that he is in the clear of and behind any backfield player. This is also to be construed as including the normal path of any player in motion behind the line as well as the line of vision between such a player and the maker of a pass (forward or backward). He shall also favor the right side (if the passer is right-handed). He will count offensive players.

Article 7   At the end of any down, the Referee may (when in doubt or at the request of a captain unless obviously unnecessary) request the linesman and his assistants to bring the yardage chains on field to determine whether the ball has reached the necessary line. See 4-5-5-a.

Article 8   Prior to each snap, the Referee is to positively check the number of the ensuing down and distance to be gained with the Linesman, signal the Back Judge when to start his watch for the timing of 25 seconds (when appropriate), and know the eligible pass receivers.

Article 9   He is primarily responsible for spotting the ball at the inbounds spot on plays from scrimmage, and should not enter a side zone to cover a runner (other than the quarterback) when the Linesman or Line Judge is in position to do so. See 15-1-11-S.N. 1.

Note: When the ball is dead near the sideline during time in, he is not to assist in a relay to the inbounds spot, unless the umpire has been remiss or delayed in doing so (15-1-10-Note and 15-3-4). In such a case, the Umpire is to spot. See Rule 2-2 and Note, in regard to using a new ball at start of second and fourth periods in case of a wet ball.

Section 3   UMPIRE

Article 1   The Umpire has primary jurisdiction over the equipment and the conduct and actions of players on the scrimmage line.

Article 2   Before the game, the Umpire with assistance of other officials shall inspect the equipment of players. He may order any changes he deems necessary to any proposed equipment which is considered dangerous or confusing (5-4). This authority extends throughout the game.

Article 3   He shall assist in relaying the ball:

(a) to the inbounds spot when it is dead near a sideline during time in when feasible (15-2-9-Note);

(b) to the previous spot after an incompletion; and

(c) to the spot of a free kick when indicated. See 15-1-11-S.N.

Article 4   The Umpire shall record:

(a) all charged team timeouts during the game;

(b) the winner of the toss; and

(c) the score.

He is to assist the Referee on decisions involving possession of the ball in close proximity to the line, after a loose ball or runner has crossed it. He and the Line Judge are to determine whether ineligible linemen illegally cross the line prior to a pass, and he must wipe a wet ball in accordance with the proper timing. He should count the offensive players on the field at the snap.

Section 4   LINESMAN

Article 1   The Linesman operates on the side of field designated by the Referee during the first half and on opposite side during the second half unless ordered otherwise. See 1-4-Note for exception.

Article 2   He is responsible for illegal motion, offside, encroaching, and any actions pertaining to scrimmage line prior to or at snap; and for covering in his side zone. See 15-1-11-S.N. 1; 15-2-9; and 15-3-4. He will count offensive players.

Article 3   Prior to the game, he shall see that his chain crew is properly instructed as to their specific duties and mechanics.

Note: Each home team appoints the official chain crew (boxman, two rodmen and alternate, drive start and forward stake indicator) subject to approval by the league office. Each member carries a working pass to that effect and it is prohibited for anyone else to work as such. The standardized yardage chains and downs box must be used and if any others are furnished this fact is to be reported to the Commissioner.

Article 4   The Linesman shall use a clamp on the chain when measuring for first down.

Article 5   The Linesman is to mark with his foot (when up with ball) the yard line touched by forward point of ball at end of each scrimmage down. At the start of each new series of downs, he and the rodmen set the yardage chains when the Referee so signals. He positively must check with the Referee as to the number of each down that is about to start.

Note: It is mandatory for Linesman to personally see that rear rod is accurately set and also to see that the forward rodman and boxman have set the safety markers for the forward rod and the previous spot, during any series of downs, as prescribed by the officials' manual.

Article 6   On his own side, he is to assist the Line Judge as to illegal motion or a shift and umpire in regard to holding or illegal use of hands on end of line (especially during kicks or passes), and know eligible pass receivers.

Article 7   He is to mark out-of-bounds spot on his side of field when within his range and is to supervise substitutions made by team located on his side of field during either half.

Note: See 15-1-11-S.N. 1; 15-2-9; and 15-3-4.

Section 5   LINE JUDGE

Article 1   The Line Judge is to operate on side of field opposite the Linesman.

Article 2   He is responsible for the timing of game. He also is responsible for illegal motion, illegal shift, and for covering in his side zone. See 15-1-11-S.N. 1 and 15-2-9. He will count offensive players.

Article 3   He is responsible for supervision of the timing and in case the game clock becomes inoperative, or for any other reason is not being operated correctly, he shall take over the official timing on the field.

Article 4   He is to time each period and (4-1-3, 4), signal the Referee when two minutes remain in a half and leave in ample time with the Field Judge to notify their respective teams of five minutes before the start of the second half.

Article 5   He shall advise the Referee when time has expired at end of a period.

Article 6   He must notify both captains, through the Referee, of the time remaining for play not more than 10 or less than five minutes before the end of each half and must signal Referee when two minutes remain in each half. In the event that the stadium clock is inoperable, he must notify both captains, through the Referee, of the time remaining for play not more than 10 or less than 5 minutes before the end of each half and must signal Referee when two minutes remain in each half.

Note: Upon inquiry of a field captain, he may state the approximate time remaining for play at any time during the game, provided he does not comply with such request more than three times during the last five minutes of either half, and provided it will not affect playing time near the end of a half (4-7-1).

Article 7   On his own side, he is to:

(a) assist the Linesman as to offside or encroaching;

(b) assist the Umpire as to holding or illegal use of hands on the end of the line (especially during kicks or passes);

(c) assist the Referee as to whether a pass is forward or backward behind the line and false starts; and

(d) be responsible for knowing the eligible pass receivers.

Article 8   He is to:

(a) mark the out-of-bounds spot of all plays on his side, when within his range (See 15-1-11-S.N. 1-3 and 15-2-9);

(b) supervise substitutions made by the team seated on his side of the field during either half (see 5-2-2);

(c) notify the home team head coach with the Field Judge five minutes before the start of the second half.

Section 6   FIELD JUDGE

Article 1   The Field Judge will operate on the same side of the field as Line Judge, 20 yards deep.

Article 2   The Field Judge shall count the number of defensive players on the field at the snap.

Article 3   He shall be responsible for all eligible receivers on his side of the field.

Article 4   After receivers have cleared line of scrimmage, the Field Judge will concentrate on action in the area between the Umpire and Back Judge.

Article 5   In addition to the specified use of the whistle by all officials (15-1-4), the Field Judge is also to use his whistle when upon his positive knowledge he knows:

(a) that ball is dead;

(b) that time is out;

(c) that time is out at the end of a down, during which a foul was signaled by a marker, no whistle has sounded in such cases; and

(d) that even in the presence of a whistle up or down field, he is to sound his whistle when players are

---

some distance from such signal. This will help prevent dead ball fouls.

Article 6   The Field Judge will assist Referee in decisions involving any catching, recovery, out of bounds spot, or illegal touching, of a loose ball, after it has crossed scrimmage line and particularly so for such actions that are out of the range of the Line Judge and Umpire. See 15-1-11-S.N. 1.

Article 7   On field-goal attempts or Try-kick attempts, the Field On field-goal attempts or Try-kick attempts, the Field Judge will station himself on the end line and cover the upright opposite the Back Judge. He, along with the Back Judge, is responsible for indication to the Referee whether the kick is high enough and through the uprights.

Section 7   **SIDE JUDGE**

Article 1   The Side Judge will operate on the same side of the field as the Head Linesman, 20 yards deep.

Article 2   The Side Judge shall count the number of defensive players on the field at the snap.

Article 3   He shall be responsible for all eligible receivers on his side of the field.

Article 4   After receivers have cleared line of scrimmage, the Side Judge will concentrate on action in the area between the Umpire and Back Judge.

Article 5   In addition to the specified use of the whistle by all officials (15-1-4), the Side Judge is also to use his whistle when upon his positive knowledge he knows:

(a) that ball is dead;

(b) that time is out;

(c) that time is out at the end of a down, during which a foul was signaled by a marker, no whistle has sounded in such cases; and

(d) that even in the presence of a whistle up or down field, he is to sound his whistle when players are some distance from such signal. This will help prevent dead ball fouls.

Article 6 The Side Judge will assist Referee in decisions involving any catching, recovery, out of bounds spot, or illegal touching, of a loose ball, after it has crossed scrimmage line and particularly so for such actions that are out of the range of the Head Linesman and Umpire.

Article 7 The Side Judge will line up in a position laterally from the Umpire on field goals and Try-kick attempts.

Section 8 **BACK JUDGE**

Article 1 The Back Judge is primarily responsible in regard to: covering kicks from scrimmage (unless a Try-kick) or forward passes crossing the defensive goal line and all such loose balls, out of the range of Umpire, Field Judge, and Linesman, noting an illegal substitution or withdrawal during dead ball with time in (see 5-2-10), and a foul signaled by a flag or cap during down. He will count defensive team.

Article 2 He is to time the intermission between the two periods of each half (4-1-2), the length of all team timeouts (4-5-1-Item 2), and the 40/25 seconds permitted Team A to put ball in play (4-6-1 and 4-6-2). He is to utilize the 40/25 second clock provided for by the home team. If this clock is inoperative he should take over the official timing of the 40/25 seconds on the field.

Article 3 In addition to the specified use of the whistle by all officials (15-1-4), the Back Judge is also to use his whistle, when upon his own positive knowledge he knows:

(a) that ball is dead;

(b) time is out; or

(c) is out at end of down, during which a foul was <u>sig-naled</u> by a flag or cap, and no whistle has sounded in such cases.

Even in the presence of a whistle upfield, he is to sound his when downfield players are some distance away from such signal, and in order to prevent dead ball fouls. He should be particularly alert for item (c).

Article 4   He shall assist the Referee in decisions involving any catching, recovery, out of bounds spot, or illegal touching, of a loose ball, after it has crossed scrimmage line and particularly so for such actions as are out of the range of the Field Judge, Linesman, and Umpire. See 15-1-11-S.N. 1. He should count the defensive players on the field at the snap.

Article 5   The Back Judge has the absolute responsibility:

(a) to instruct kicker and/or placekicker that "kickoff" *must* be made by placekick or dropkick.

(b) that the height of the tee (artificial or natural) used for the kickoff conforms to the governing rules.

Note: He is to notify the visiting team at least five minutes before the start of the second half.

Section 9   **INSTANT REPLAY**

The League will employ a system of Referee Replay Review to aid officiating for reviewable plays as defined below. Prior to the two-minute warning of each half, a Coaches' Challenge System will be in effect. After the two-minute warning of each half, and throughout any overtime period, a Referee Review will be initiated by a Replay Assistant from a Replay Booth comparable to the location of the coaches' booth or Press Box. The following procedures will be used:

Coaches' Challenge. In each game, a team will be permitted two challenges that will initiate Referee Replay reviews. Each challenge will require the use of a team timeout. If a challenge is upheld, the timeout will be restored to the challenging team. A challenge will only be restored if a team is successful on both of its challenges, in which case it shall be awarded a third challenge, but a fourth challenge will not be permitted under any circumstances. No challenges will be recognized from a team that has exhausted its timeouts. A team that is out of timeouts or has used all of its available challenges may not attempt to initiate an additional challenge.

Penalty: For initiating a challenge when all of a team's timeouts have been exhausted or when all of its available challenges have been used: Loss of 15 yards.

Replay Assistant's Request for Review. After the two-minute warning of each half, and throughout any overtime period, any Referee Review will be initiated by a Replay Assistant. There is no limit to the number of Referee Reviews that may be initiated by the Replay Assistant. His ability to initiate a review will be unrelated to the number of timeouts that either team has remaining, and no timeout will be charged for any review initiated by the Replay Assistant.

Reviews by Referee. All Replay Reviews will be conducted by the Referee on a field-level monitor after consultation with the other covering official(s), prior to review. A decision will be reversed only when the Referee has *indisputable visual evidence* available to him that warrants the change.

Time Limit. Each review will be a maximum of 60 seconds in length, timed from when the Referee begins his review of the replay at the field-level monitor.

Reviewable Plays. The Replay System will cover the following play situations only:

(a) Plays governed by Sideline, Goal Line, End Zone, and End Line:
1. Scoring Plays, including a runner breaking the plane of the goal line.
2. Pass complete/incomplete/intercepted at sideline, goal line, end zone, and end line.
3. Runner/receiver in or out of bounds.
4. Recovery of loose ball in or out of bounds.

(b) Passing Plays:
1. Pass ruled complete/incomplete/intercepted in the field of play.
2. Touching of a forward pass by an ineligible receiver.
3. Touching of a forward pass by a defensive player.
4. Quarterback (Passer) forward pass or fumble.
5. Illegal forward pass beyond line of scrimmage.
6. Illegal forward pass after change of possession.
7. Forward or backward pass thrown from behind line of scrimmage.

(c) Other reviewable plays:
1. Runner ruled not down by defensive contact.
2. Runner ruled down by defensive contact when the recovery of a fumble by an opponent or a teammate occurs in the action that happens following the fumble.
3. Ruling of incomplete pass when the recovery of a passer's fumble by an opponent or a teammate occurs in the action following a fumble.
4. Ruling of a loose ball out of bounds when it is recovered in the field of play by an opponent or a teammate in the action after the ball hits the ground.

Note 1: If the ruling of down by contact or imcomplete pass is changed, the ball belongs to the recovering player at the spot of the recovery of the fumble, and any advance is nullified.

Note 2: If the Referee does not have indisputable visual evidence as to which player recovered the <u>loose ball</u>, the ruling <u>on the field</u> will stand.

Note 3: This does not apply to complete/incomplete passes, or the ruling of forward progress.

5. Forward progress with respect to a first down.
6. Touching of a kick.
7. A field-goal or Try attempt that crosses below or above the crossbar, inside or outside the uprights when it is lower than the top of the uprights, or touches anything.
8. Number of players <u>at the snap</u>.
9. Illegal forward handoff.

Note: Non-reviewable plays include but are not limited to:

1. Status of the clock
2. Proper down
3. Penalty administration
4. Runner ruled down by defensive contact (not involving fumbles)
5. Forward progress not relating to first down or goal line
6. Recovery of a loose ball <u>that does not involve a boundary line or the end</u> zone.
7. Field-goal or Try attempts that cross above either upright without touching anything.
8. Inadvertent Whistle

Sudden-Death
Procedures

Rule 16

Sudden-Death Procedures

Section 1   **SUDDEN-DEATH PROCEDURES**

Article 1   The sudden-death system of determining the winner shall prevail when the score is tied at the end of the regulation playing time of *all* preseason and regular-season *NFL games.* Under this system, the team scoring first during overtime play herein provided for, shall be the winner of the game and the game is automatically ended upon any score (including a safety) or when a score is awarded by the Referee for a palpably unfair act.

Article 2   At the end of regulation playing time, the Referee shall immediately toss a coin at the center of the field, in accordance with rules pertaining to a usual pregame toss (4-2-2). The visiting team captain is to again call the toss.

Article 3   Following an intermission of no more than three minutes after the end of the regular game, there shall be a maximum of one 15-minute period. If neither team has scored, the game shall result in a tie. Each team shall be entitled to two timeouts, and if there is an excess timeout, the usual rules shall apply (4-5). The general provisions for the fourth quarter of a game shall apply, except all replay reviews will be initiated by the replay assistant. Coaches' challenges will not be allowed.

Article 4   For postseason games, following a coin flip (Article 2 above) and an intermission of no more than three minutes after the end of the regular game, the following shall apply:

(a) Both teams must have the opportunity to possess the ball once during the extra period, unless the team that receives the opening kickoff (Team B) scores a touchdown on its initial possession, in which case it is the winner, or Team A scores a safety on Team B's initial possession, in which case Team A is the winner.

(b) If the team that possesses the ball first scores a field goal on its initial possession, the other team (Team A) shall have the opportunity to possess the ball. If Team A scores a touchdown on its possession, it is the winner. If the score is tied after Team A's possession, the team next scoring by any method shall be the winner.

(c) If the score is tied at the end of a 15-minute overtime period, or if Team B's initial possession has not ended, another overtime period will begin, and play will continue, regardless of how many 15-minute periods are necessary.

(d) Between each overtime period, there shall be a two-minute intermission, but there shall be no halftime intermission after the second period. At the beginning of the third overtime period, the captain who lost the coin toss prior to the first overtime period shall have the first choice of the two privileges in Rule 4, Section 2, Article 2, unless the team that won the coin toss deferred.

(e) At the end of the first and third extra periods, etc., teams must change goals in accordance with Rule 4, Section 2, Article 3.

(f) A player is in possession when he is in firm grip and control of the ball inbounds (3-2-7). The defense gains possession when it catches, intercepts, or recovers a loose ball.

(g) The opportunity to possess applies only during kicking plays. A kickoff is the opportunity to possess for the receiving team. If the kicking team legally recovers the kick, the receiving team is considered to have had its opportunity. A punt or field goal that crosses the line of scrimmage and is muffed by the receiving team is considered to be an opportunity to possess for the receiving team. Normal touching rules by the kicking team apply.

(h) Each team is entitled to three timeouts during a half. If there is an excess timeout the usual rules shall apply (4-5).

(i) At the end of a second overtime period, timing rules shall apply as at the end of the first half. At the end of a fourth overtime period, timing rules shall apply as at the end of the fourth quarter.

(j) All replay reviews will be initiated by the replay assistant. Coaches' challenges will not be allowed.

Article 5 Disqualified player(s) shall not re-enter during any extra period or periods in the preseason, regular season, and postseason.

Article 6 Except as provided for above, all other general and specific rules shall apply during any extra period or periods in the preseason, regular season, and postseason.

Emergencies, Unfair Acts

Rule 17

Emergencies, Unfair Acts

Section 1   **EMERGENCIES**

Article 1   If any non-player, including photographers, reporters, employees, police or spectators, enters the field of play or end zones, and in the judgment of an official said party or parties interfere with the play, the Referee, after consulting his crew (12-3-3 and 15-1-6), shall enforce any such penalty or score as the interference warrants.

Article 2   If spectators enter the field and/or interfere with the progress of the game in such a manner that in the opinion of the Referee the game cannot continue, he shall declare time out. In such a case he shall record the number of the down, distance to be gained, and position of ball on field. He shall also secure from the line judge the playing time remaining and record it. He shall then order the home club through its management to have the field cleared, and when it is cleared and order restored and the safety of the spectators, players and officials is assured to the satisfaction of the Referee, the game must continue even if it is necessary to use lights.

Article 3   If the game must be called due to a state or municipal law, or by darkness if no lights are available, an immediate report shall be made to the Commissioner by the home club, visiting club and officials. On receipt of all reports the Commissioner shall make a decision which will be final.

Article 4   The NFL affirms the position that in most circumstances all regular-season and postseason games should be played to their conclusion. If, in the opinion of appropriate League authorities, it is impossible to begin or continue a game due to an emergency, or a game is deemed to be imminently threatened by any such emergency (e.g., severely inclement weather, lightning, flooding, power failure), the following procedures (Articles 5 through 11) will serve as guidelines for the Commissioner and/or his duly appointed representatives. The Commissioner has the authority to review the circumstances of each emergency and to adjust the following procedures in whatever manner he deems appropriate. If, in the Commissioner's opinion, it is reasonable to project that the resumption of an interrupted game would not change its ultimate result or adversely affect any other inter-team competitive issue, he is empowered to terminate the game.

Article 5   The League employees vested with the authority to define emergencies under these procedures are the Commissioner, designated representatives from his League office staff, and the game Referee. In those instances where neither the Commissioner nor his designated representative is in attendance at a game, the Referee will have sole authority; provided, however, that if a Referee delays the beginning of or interrupts a game for a significant period of time due to an emergency, he must make every effort to contact the Commissioner or the Commissioner's designated representative for consultation. In all cases of significant delay, the League authorities will consult with the management of the participating clubs and will attempt to obtain appropriate information from outside sources, if applicable (e.g., weather bureau, police).

Article 6   If, because of an emergency, a regular-season or postseason game is not started at its scheduled time and cannot be played at any later time that same day, the game nevertheless must be played on a subsequent date to be determined by the Commissioner.

Article 7   If there is deemed to be a threat of an emergency that may occur during the playing of a game (e.g., an incoming tropical storm), the starting time of such game will not be moved to an earlier time unless there is clearly sufficient time to make an orderly change.

Article 8   If, under emergency circumstances, an interrupted regular-season or post-season game cannot be completed on the same day, such game will be rescheduled by the Commissioner and resumed at that point.

Article 9   In instances under these emergency procedures which require the Commissioner to reschedule a regular-season game, he will make every effort to set the game for no later than two days after its originally scheduled date, and he will attempt to schedule the game at its original site. If unable to do so, he will schedule it at the nearest available facility. If it is impossible to schedule the game within two days after its original date, the Commissioner will attempt to schedule it on the Tuesday of the next calendar week in which the two involved clubs play other clubs (or each other). Further, the Commissioner will keep in mind the potential for competitive inequities if one or both of the involved clubs has already been scheduled for a game following the Tuesday of that week (e.g., Thanksgiving).

Article 10   If an emergency interrupts a postseason game and such game cannot be resumed on that same date, the Commissioner will make every effort to arrange for its completion as soon as possible. If unable to schedule the game at the same site, he will select an appropriate alternate site. He will terminate the game short of completion only if in his judgment the continuation of the game would not be normally expected to alter the ultimate result.

Article 11   In all instances where a game is resumed after interruption, either on the same date or a subsequent date, the resumption will begin at the point at which the game was interrupted. At the time of interruption, the Referee will call timeout and he will make a record of the following: the team possessing the ball, the direction in which its offense was headed, position of the ball on the field, down, distance, period, time remaining in the period, and any other pertinent information required for an efficient and equitable resumption of play.

Section 2   **EXTRAORDINARILY UNFAIR ACTS**

Article 1   The Commissioner has the sole authority to investigate and take appropriate disciplinary and/or corrective measures if any club action, non-participant interference, or calamity occurs in an NFL game which he deems so extraordinarily unfair or outside the accepted tactics encountered in professional football that such action has a major effect on the result of the game.

Article 2   The authority and measures provided for in this entire Section 2 do not constitute a protest machinery for NFL clubs to avail themselves of in the event a dispute arises over the result of a game. The investigation called for in this Section 2 will be conducted solely on the Commissioner's initiative to review an act or occurrence that he deems so extraordinary or unfair that the result of the game in question would be inequitable to one of the participating teams. The Commissioner will not apply his authority in cases of complaints by clubs concerning judgmental errors or routine errors of omission by game officials. Games involving such complaints will continue to stand as completed.

Article 3 The Commissioner's powers under this Section 2 include the imposition of monetary fines and draft-choice forfeitures, suspension of persons involved in unfair acts, and, if appropriate, the reversal of a game's result or the rescheduling of a game, either from the beginning or from the point at which the extraordinary act occurred. In the event of rescheduling a game, the Commissioner will be guided by the procedures specified in Rule 17, Section 1, Articles 5 through 11, above. In all cases, the Commissioner will conduct a full investigation, including the opportunity for hearings, use of game videotape, and any other procedure he deems appropriate.

Guidelines
for Captains

Rule 18

Guidelines for Captains

Section 1   **GUIDELINES FOR CAPTAINS**

Article 1   One hour and thirty minutes prior to kickoff: Respective coaches designate the captain(s)—a maximum of six per team.

Article 2   Coin toss:

(a) Up to six captains per team can participate in the coin toss ceremony; only one captain from the visiting team (or captain designated by Referee if there is no home team) can declare the choice of coin toss.

(b) The team that won the toss may then have only one captain declare its option.

(c) The team that lost the coin toss may then have only one captain declare its option.

Article 3   Choice on Penalty Option: Only one captain is permitted to indicate the team's penalty option.

Article 4   Change of Captains:

(a) The coach has prerogative of informing Referee when he wishes to make a change in team captains; or

(b) A captain who is leaving can inform the Referee which player will act as captain in his place when he is substituted for; or

(c) When a captain leaves the game, the incoming substitute is permitted to inform the Referee which player the respective coach has designated as captain.

Note: A captain on the field has no authority to request a change of fellow team captain when that captain remains on the field.

Penalty
Summary

Distance Penalties

Loss of Five Yards

Loss of 10 Yards

Loss of Half Distance to Goal Line

Ball Placed on 1-Yard Line

Withdrawal Penalties

Disqualification Penalties

Disqualification always occurs in combination with a 15-yard penalty.
Exceptions to distance penalties:

Both teams committing disqualifying fouls (double foul)................14-3-1

Distance being declined 14-6

Loss of 15 Yards

Flagrant striking, kicking, or kneeing an opponent or striking him
on head or neck with heel, back or side of hand, wrist, elbow, or
forearm 12-2-1

Flagrant roughing of kicker...12-2-6

Flagrant roughing of passer 12-2-13

Flagrant unsportsmanlike conduct by players 12-3-1

Player using a helmet as a weapon..12-2-15

Disqualified player returning (exclusion from field enclosure).................5-2-7

Suspended player illegally returning...5-2-7

Loss of Ball Penalties

Ball being behind necessary line at end of fourth down 7-1-1

Kickers first touching kick (not a free kick) in field of play 9-2-2

Interfering with fair catch (also fair catch allowed) 10-1-1

Disqualification for Entire Game

Repeat violation by player wearing or displaying illegal equipment 5-4-9

Charged Timeout Penalties

Actions to converve time...4-7-1

Taking timeout for injured player during last two minutes of either
half (withdrawal only when fourth timeout—also loss of five when
fifth or more) 4-5-4

Time Penalty

Actions to conserve time 4-7-1

Fouling by defense, illegal touching or fair-catch interfering by offense
or fouling by both teams at end of half during play in which time
expires (extend quarter)..4-8-2

Replay Penalties

Team B fouling on Try which fails 11-3-3

Committing double foul unless dead-ball fouls by both teams after ball
is dead, the one only disqualifying foul is by Team B ....14-1-8 and 9;
14-3-1; and 14-3-2

Scoring Penalties

Try Awarded

Score Awarded

Touchdown Awarded

Safety

Score Not Allowed

Unsuccessful Try

New Series Penalties

Combination Penalties

Loss of Down and Five

Loss of Down and 10

Loss of Ball and 15

Touchback

Score, Distance or Disqualification

Miscellaneous Situations

Safety

Ball in possession of team behind or out of bounds behind own goal
line and impetus which sent it in touch came from:

Kickoff Out of Bounds Between Goal Lines

Ball Remains Dead

Ball Dead Immediately

Penalty Enforced From Goal Line

Penalty Enforced on Next Free Kick

Official Signals

1
TOUCHDOWN,
FIELD GOAL, OR
SUCCESSFUL TRY
Both arms extended
above head.

2
SAFETY
Palms together
above head.

3
FIRST DOWN
Arm pointed toward
defensive team's goal.

4
CROWD NOISE, DEAD BALL, OR
NEUTRAL ZONE ESTABLISHED
One arm above head with an
open hand. With fist closed:
FOURTH DOWN.

5
BALL ILLEGALLY
TOUCHED, KICKED,
OR BATTED
Fingertips tap both
shoulders.

6
TIMEOUT
Hands crisscrossed above
head. Same signal followed
by placing one hand on top
of cap: REFEREE'S TIMEOUT.
Same signal followed by
arm swung at side:
TOUCHBACK.

7
NO TIMEOUT OR TIME IN
WITH WHISTLE
Full arm circled to simulate
moving clock.

8
DELAY OF GAME,
OFFENSE/DEFENSE,
OR EXCESS TIMEOUT
Folded arms.

9
FALSE START, ILLEGAL
FORMATION, KICKOFF OR
SAFETY KICK OUT OF BOUNDS,
OR KICKING TEAM PLAYER VOL-
UNTARILY OUT OF BOUNDS
DURING A PUNT
Forearms rotated over and
over in front of body.

10
PERSONAL FOUL
One wrist striking the other
above head. Same signal
followed by swinging leg:
ROUGHING KICKER. Same
signal followed by raised
arm swinging forward:
ROUGHING PASSER.
Same signal followed by
grasping facemask:
MAJOR FACEMASK.

11
HOLDING
Grasping one wrist, the fist
clenched, in front of chest.

12
ILLEGAL USE OF HANDS, ARMS,
OR BODY
Grasping one wrist, the
hand open and facing
forward, in front of chest

13
**PENALTY REFUSED,
INCOMPLETE PASS, PLAY OVER,
OR MISSED GOAL**
Hands shifted in
horizontal plane.

14
**PASS JUGGLED INBOUNDS AND
CAUGHT OUT OF BOUNDS**
Hands up and down in
front of chest (following
incomplete pass signal).

15
ILLEGAL FORWARD PASS
One hand waved behind
back followed by loss of
down signal (23) when
appropriate.

16
**INTENTIONAL GROUNDING
OF PASS**
Parallel arms waved in a
diagonal plane across body.
Followed by loss of down
signal (23).

17
**INTERFERENCE WITH FORWARD
PASS
OR FAIR CATCH**
Hands open and extended
forward from shoulders
with hands vertical.

18
INVALID FAIR-CATCH SIGNAL
One hand waved
above head.

19
**INELIGIBLE RECEIVER OR INELI-
GIBLE MEMBER OF KICKING
TEAM DOWNFIELD**
Right hand touching
top of cap.

20
ILLEGAL CONTACT
One open hand extended
forward.

21
**OFFSIDE, ENCROACHMENT, OR
NEUTRAL ZONE INFRACTION**
Hands on hips.

22
ILLEGAL MOTION AT SNAP
Horizontal arc with one
hand.

23
LOSS OF DOWN
Both hands held behind
head.

24
**INTERLOCKING INTERFERENCE,
PUSHING, OR HELPING RUNNER**
Pushing movement of
hands to front with arms
downward.

25
TOUCHING A FORWARD PASS OR SCRIMMAGE KICK
Diagonal motion of one hand across another.

26
UNSPORTSMANLIKE CONDUCT
Arms outstretched, palms down.

27
ILLEGAL CUT
Both hands striking front of thigh. **ILLEGAL BLOCK BELOW THE WAIST:** One hand striking front of thigh preceded by personal foul signal (10). **CHOP BLOCK:** Both hands striking side of thighs preceded by personal foul signal (10). **CLIPPING:** One hand striking back of calf preceded by personal foul signal (10).

28
ILLEGAL CRACKBACK
Strike of an open right hand against the right mid thigh preceded by personal foul signal (10).

29
PLAYER DISQUALIFIED
Ejection signal.

30
TRIPPING
Repeated action of right foot in back of left heel.

31
UNCATCHABLE
FORWARD PASS
Palm of right hand held
parallel to ground above
head and moved back
and forth.

32
ILLEGAL SUBSTITUTION,
12 MEN IN OFFENSIVE
HUDDLE, OR TOO MANY MEN ON
THE FIELD
Both hands on top of head.

33
FACEMASK
Grasping mask with
one hand.

34
ILLEGAL SHIFT
Horizontal arcs with
two hands.

35
RESET PLAY CLOCK –
25 SECONDS
Pump one arm vertically.

36
RESET PLAY CLOCK –
40 SECONDS
Pump two arms vertically.